LEVIATHAN EXPOSED

Overcoming the Hidden Schemes of a Demonic King

ROBERT HOTCHKIN

LEVIATHAN EXPOSED

Overcoming the Hidden Schemes of a Demonic King

ROBERT HOTCHKIN

LEVIATHAN EXPOSED

Published and distributed by:

XP Publishing
XP Ministries
PO Box 1017
Maricopa, AZ 85139
XPministries.com
For worldwide distribution

ISBN: 978-1-621661-76-4

ENDORSEMENTS

"My friend Robert Hotchkin has done a masterful job of exposing one of the most subtle and fierce, dark, diabolical enemies of our lives. Good, clear communications are vital and a necessary key to having a growing, maturing relationship – in every sphere of life and ministry. Leviathan is a conniving demonic spirit that aims to twist communications. It is time that we learn the signs, step to the plate, and win this battle!"

James W. Goll
Founder of ElNetwork
International Best Selling Author

"As believers, we have an enemy whose sole intent is to steal, kill, and destroy (John 10:10). When we are aware of his schemes (2 Corinthians 2:11) we realize that our real fight is not against fellow believers, and that God has given all of us powerful weapons that will overcome every plan of the enemy to divide the Church. Robert Hotchkin has written a compelling account, filled with real life examples of how believers can disentangle themselves from the web of communication gone awry. If you have ever been caught in the painful place of twisted communication or false accusation, this book will give you the tools you need to get free."

Stacey Campbell
RevivalNOW Ministries, revivalnow.com, Canada

"If you're like me, every once in a while you find yourself in the middle of a great big mess in which everyone is arguing or feeling hurt by someone else in your family, church, or home group. That has happened to me so many times through the years, I can't count. In the midst of one of these seasons of attack, my wife will often exclaim, 'This is an attack by the devil!' And I'm ashamed to say my first response has been, 'No, this isn't an attack. This is *so-and-so* being stubborn again.'

"What a STUPID thing for me to say! Of course it's an attack, by SATAN, often using his most powerful agent, Leviathan, a snake of all snakes. A twister of words, motives and actions, and even health issues. If one demon can be more evil than another, Leviathan wins one of the top 'evil' awards. By it, churches, ministries, marriages, and relationships are destroyed while 'it' remains anonymous.

"In this crucially important book, *Leviathan Exposed*, Robert Hotchkin unravels this twisted serpent and the way it works. But far more importantly, Robert lays out keys, methods, and amazing strategies – all from God's Word – to defeat and destroy the works of this serpent. GET THIS BOOK! Pass it out to all your friends, ministry heads, teachers, students, and loved ones. And more importantly, read it yourself! Then TAKE ACTION. Do what it says and watch this evil snake-spirit slither away in utter defeat! Again, PLEASE READ THIS BOOK!"

STEVE SHULTZ
The Elijah List

"As I read Robert's book, *Leviathan Exposed*, my thoughts and memories were jarred and my eyes were opened. Where was your book, Robert, 30 years ago? Where were you three years ago when two women met in my office to settle a difference and, refusing to 'hear' one another, left with anger, disagreement, and twisted, false impressions that have left a rift to this day? 'That's what was going on!' I exclaimed, as clarity came. Now I realize they were not just being stubborn, but something else was at work behind the scenes. "I was reminded of the Scripture verse in which Hosea said, 'My people are destroyed for lack of knowledge' (Hosea 4:6). That sad reality continues to exist today as believers find themselves being captured into reacting to others' communication with misunderstanding, frustration, exasperation, anger and, in many instances, separation and broken relationships. Unity and trust is destroyed because we have lacked knowledge about the real culprit – the destroyer himself – and blamed one another.

"Many times, when just not able to pinpoint the cause of ructions and destructions in specific situations, I have cried out to God, 'Lord, paint the dragon red,' and He has done just that with clarity. Now, thankfully, that is exactly what the Spirit has enabled Robert to do – paint this dragon red and make the exposure of this destructive Leviathan spirit so brilliantly clear that we can stop being trapped by it at the very beginning of the attack, even taking the authority that is ours to trample on snakes and scorpions and to overcome all the power of the enemy, knowing nothing will harm us (Luke 10:19).

"This is such an anointed book! It's not all about demon chasing; it's full of compassion, revelation, and understanding. Robert gives powerful keys for overcoming the works of Leviathan as it is dismantled and demolished to nothing when you discover it in your midst."

MARY AUDREY RAYCROFT
Teaching Pastor, Catch The Fire, Toronto,
Founder of Releasers of Life Equipping Ministry

"In this powerful book, Robert makes a clear and compelling case to equip every believer to partner with God in seeing the schemes of the enemy defeated. This is a must read for anyone desiring a life free from the effects of miscommunication, misunderstanding, and offense. The teaching is deep, yet accessible, and presented in a way as to inspire you to go deeper in your faith. As church leaders we have personally benefited from reading Robert's book and have found new strategies for helping the people entrusted to us overcome their relational challenges."

TOM AND ABI ALLSOP
Associate Pastors, Catch the Fire, England

"*Leviathan Exposed* helps you to not only recognize the enemy but to learn how to strategize and defeat him at every turn! Life and death are in the power of our mouths, and our words set and create thought patterns. There are valuable keys embedded in this book that will help you to unlock areas within your own life. This book will be a most valuable tool in your arsenal, as it reveals many of the enemy's ploys, plots, and schemes to ready you to engage and destroy what the enemy intends to use for your destruction."

ANGELA GREENIG
Angela Greenig Ministries, Kingdom Invasion Media
angelagreenig.com

"I love this book! I have successfully battled with the spirit of Leviathan on many occasions and experienced extraordinary miracles through those victories. Yet in *Leviathan Exposed*, Robert Hotchkin unveils page after page of amazing biblical insights that I had not yet seen. After reading this, I feel so much more informed and empowered to take this beast down and free the Body from his tyranny. Well done, Robert!"

KATIE SOUZA
Healing Your Soul – Real Keys to the Miraculous
Prison Outreach of Expected End Ministries

"In *Leviathan Exposed*, Robert Hotchkin has not only identified a major spirit that is challenging the Body of Christ, but he has also revealed how to overcome it! This book is an absolute necessity for anyone in leadership because, whether you know it or not, you have come across this spirit! Gaining understanding on this subject is going to allow the Church to take territory that has, up to this point, been controlled by the enemy. *Leviathan Exposed* delivers a HUGE blow to the kingdom of darkness!"

BRAD CARTER
Lead Pastor, Kingdom Builders Ministries
kingdombuildersnc.org

"This book could not have come at a better time! It is of great importance that this demonic spirit be exposed right now. We have experienced the spirit of Leviathan up close and seen the damage it does to families, friends, and churches. Thank you, Robert, for writing this important book. Thank you for exposing one of the strongest demonic kings and its workings so that we can be awakened and prepared in a time for us all to arise and work together to bring the Kingdom of God to the world. What a gift and blessing this book will be for those who read it and share it. *Leviathan Exposed* will bring unity, peace, and understanding. Let us stay close to our Father. Let us stay close to one another."

PETER AND ANNA FAGERHOV
Lead Pastors, Nordanstigs Kristna Center, Sweden

"Practical, yet deeply biblical, Robert's new book *Leviathan Exposed* is a rich vault of revelation around the often mistaught and misunderstood realm of spiritual warfare. Robert's ability to center around what really matters is what makes this book a great tool to overcome the enemy. His emphasis on fighting from victory instead of for victory is a revelation every believer needs to understand. Full of helpful insight into relationships, conflict, and how Leviathan works, this book will help you see HOW to posture yourself in times of spiritual conflict and how to practically see the enemy defeated. It is a must for every believer to read. Victorious and full of hope, *Leviathan Exposed* will stir faith to see your breakthrough and enjoy a life free of fear of the enemy!"

JULIAN ADAMS
Frequentsee Trust
A prophetic ministry equipping people
for revival and reformation

"As I began reading *Leviathan Exposed,* I was reminded of a similar work by Francis Frangipane titled *Exposing the Jezebel Spirit.* Robert's book is equally informative and objective at exposing a spirit that hinders much of what the Church is doing today. With the exposure, he provides the tools to rid it from your midst. Thank you, Robert. This book ought to be a requirement for all christian colleges and ministry schools."

RANDY DEMAIN
Kingdom Revelation Ministries

DEDICATED TO

Holy Spirit; the clearest, most loving and best communicator I know. Thank You for helping me to learn and discern. You are an amazing Teacher, Counselor, and Friend. I am so very grateful for You.

My friend and mentor, Patricia King. I am a better communicator, leader, and person because of what you have modeled and all that you have poured into me over the years.

And of course, my wonderful wife. Thank you, Yu-Ree, for loving me and the Lord so much; and for being so understanding about the many hours I spent with Him and my computer instead of you during the writing and creation of this book.

TABLE OF CONTENTS

FOREWORD

Patricia King

Leviathan is an evil, twisted, demonic serpent that is sent to steal, kill, and destroy. Left on its own, it will destroy relationships, strip people of confidence, wound hearts, and kill ministries and reputations. I am not afraid of battle and am convinced that light invades and overpowers darkness. I have been acquainted with spiritual warfare over the years, and have always believed the word that Jesus proclaimed, "Behold, I have given you authority to tread on serpents and scorpions, and over all the power of the enemy, and nothing will injure you" (Luke 10:19). As a result, the Lord has led us as a ministry with confidence and peace through the battlefields. The outcome is always good if you follow Him.

In most cases, the enemy uses unsuspecting people to wage his warfare, and I have seen many become pawns in his hands over the years. I have observed ministry leaders and ministries worldwide being attacked by a Leviathan spirit; our own ministry experienced such an attack. This spirit is not a respecter of persons or of geographical locations, and neither does it matter to it whether you have great or little influence.

Our battle is not against flesh and blood, but against the rulers, powers, and forces of darkness (Ephesians 6:12). I have seen this brutal spirit take advantage of unsuspecting individuals, using them to create swirls in communication that escalate into destruction without reprieve or intervention. From numerous directions the swirls intensified and moved into bitter and painful accusations on many fronts. Every situation I have observed in which Leviathan was involved was brutal, yet it was being fueled by individuals who were normally very loving, committed Christians. I have observed the enemy taking advantage in fury, and in the midst of it, many have been devastated and deeply hurt.

As a leader, it is hard to unpack the numerous twisted elements of the battle. People's pain and anger need to be dealt with. Every individual involved needs to be carefully listened to and aided so they can embrace repentance and healing – emotionally, relationally, and spiritually, then be brought into a place where they are safe from the assault of this deadly enemy. My greatest prayer when invited to help and lead in these battles has been, "Lord, what does love look like in this situation? What does Your redemptive purpose look like in this battle? Teach me to pursue, overtake, and recover all."

When dealing with these assaults, I would cry out constantly, "Oh, God, I need to be as wise as a serpent and as harmless as a dove. Help me walk in pure love in every situation. Help me to help others, and keep my team and those I love safe from the horrific deception and brutal attack of this wicked spirit. Grant me wisdom … I need wisdom!"

Through fasting, prayer, and waiting on God, in every situation God has guided us through the minefields. We have learned to listen to One voice. Every other voice in the midst of such battles needs to be silenced, as there is always a measure of distortion in most involved due to the influence of this spirit's attack. Some have been deeply hurt in the process as they heard things that were not said and perceived motives that were not intended. I've observed the enemy over and over taking advantage of some legitimate problems that needed to be carefully addressed with wisdom and Spirit-led discipline. When a Leviathan spirit is involved, it can all go south quickly.

I hate seeing people hurt, and so does God. He is calling forth an army who will confront and overcome this spirit in truth, righteousness, and love. He wants to give every individual who is under assault the victory that He secured for us 2,000 years ago on the cross.

Any battle you find yourself in will potentially strengthen and promote you at the end of the process, if you walk with the Lord in it. My prayer for you, if you are battling this spirit or helping others to battle it, is that you will find the amazing triumph and victory that is yours through Christ by covenant. God is with you! You are an overcomer!

Robert Hotchkin has written this brilliant resource for you based on valuable insights he and our team have gleaned from the Lord as we encountered this spirit and walked with God towards victory. I believe this book will give you insight into how this spirit operates and will give you keys and strategies on how to win every battle. Christ in us has overcome all. We, in Christ, are safe and secure. We win! You win! For God has "crushed the heads of Leviathan" (Psalm 74:14).

PATRICIA KING
Founder, Patricia King Ministries

1

LEVIATHAN: A GLOBAL ASSAULT

Every time you turn on the news there seems to be yet another story about a conflict, attack, murder, misunderstanding, or some other sort of turmoil – whether it's in a home, a school, a church, a business, a theatre, a courtroom, a government building, or on a battlefield. Individuals are in conflict. Regions are in conflict. Nations are in conflict. Impatience, irritation, and offense seem to be everywhere. Even when people do take the time to meet and try to resolve things, division and dissension are all too often the result. We seem to have so little grace, peace, and patience for one another any more – even in the Body of Christ. It is not by chance that this is happening; that miscommunication, misunderstanding, chaos, conflict, disagreement, and discord are all on the rise. There is a force behind it, a spirit – the spirit of Leviathan.

Leviathan is a wicked and powerful spirit that has been loosed into the earth to twist and pervert communications and understanding with the goal of destroying alliances, unions and relationships. Its assault is global. There is not one area of the world or our lives that it will not try to infiltrate and bring devastation and destruction to. Make no mistake about it: We are at war; we have an enemy, and Leviathan is one of his stealthiest and most devastating agents.

The good news, though, is that we also have a Savior. He has overcome on our behalf. And He will teach us how to lay hold of His victory in every area Leviathan attempts to assault.

We never want to so focus on the enemy that we lose sight of the Savior. In a season of warfare, however, it is important to understand what we are up against so that we can seek the Lord for His guidance and strategies on how to overcome. Yes, Leviathan has been loosed on a global level to wreak havoc and bring destruction, but fear not, because the Lord has loosed powerful weapons of warfare that will allow us to conquer and destroy Leviathan. As you read this book you will come to understand what this spirit is, how it works, and how to wield the weapons of warfare that the Lord has given us to render all of Leviathan's machinations null and void.

There are two areas, or "territories," that the enemy assaults. The territory we have, and the territory we are coming into.

THE TERRITORY WE HAVE

John 10:10 makes it clear that the thief comes to steal, kill, and destroy. Those are Jesus' words, so we need to heed them. I believe what He wants us to see is that if we have already obtained territory (i.e., a sphere of influence or existing relationships and alliances in our personal life, marriage, ministry, business, etc.) the enemy will try to disturb, disrupt, and destroy those areas. We need to be watchful – not afraid, but aware – knowing that the

We never want to so focus on the enemy that we lose sight of the Savior. In a season of warfare, however, it is important to understand what we are up against so that we can seek the Lord for His guidance and strategies on how to overcome.

enemy wants to tempt, trick, or deceive us into giving up or giving back the ground we have taken. When we discern that he is in our midst, it is time to unsheathe our weapons and put him in his place. Not by our might or strength, but by cooperating with the leading of the Holy Spirit, always certain of the victory that He is guiding us into. Every battle is an opportunity for triumph, and every triumph expands our sphere of influence and increases our operative authority in those areas.

THE TERRITORY WE ARE COMING INTO

When Israel entered the Promised Land they encountered one battle after another. In fact, the Lord's people faced more than ten times as many battles once they were *in* the Promised Land as they did on their way to it (Joshua 12). This was not by chance, nor was it because the enemy took them by surprise. It was because God wanted to raise up warriors and overcomers by mentoring them in how to co-labor with Him to see every battle won and every promise fully possessed and occupied. It was all part of His plan. It works the same way today. As the Lord leads us into new realms of authority in the spirit, the enemy puts up a fight to try to discourage us. Like the old saying goes: "New level. New devil."

But do not be afraid or discouraged, for the Lord your God is with you *wherever* you go (Joshua 1:9). The enemy cannot keep you from what God has for you. The Lord promises this in Genesis 28:15 when He declares, "I will be with you constantly until I have finished giving you everything I have promised" (NLT). It is all simply spiritual resistance training – strengthening our faith muscles so that we can have even greater impact for the Kingdom in the earth.

Christ has given us victory over every work of the enemy, including Leviathan. For those of you who are in a battle with this spirit right now, I want to remind you that you have the victory and you will see the spoils. I declare over each of you:

As you read this book, you will receive the weapons and tools you need to triumph over Leviathan and take even more ground for the Kingdom. Get ready to see a shift in your life. From tension and turmoil to tenacity and triumph. From chaos and confusion to clear communication. From misunderstanding and misinterpretation to multiplied impact and blessing. From broken relationships and alliances to fortified friendships and strengthened unions. It is all about to turn around for you. Breakthrough is coming. Victory is here, and the spoils are spilling forth. Territory that Leviathan has taken will be recovered. There will be recompense. It is time to see the shift!

2

THE SPIRIT OF LEVIATHAN

Have you ever found yourself in a situation where no matter what you said, it seemed to be misinterpreted? And the more you tried to explain yourself, the more it seemed to stir up misunderstanding, confusion, anger, hurt feelings, and offense? Well, that is all an indication that Leviathan is at work.

Leviathan is a high-level demonic spirit that works to twist communication, create misunderstanding, and damage or break relationship. It is mentioned several times in the Bible. The following passages provide key insights that can help us understand what this spirit is and how it works.

Let's first look at Isaiah 27:1:

In that day the LORD will punish Leviathan the fleeing serpent, with His fierce and great and mighty sword, even Leviathan the twisted serpent; and He will kill the dragon who lives in the sea.

Here we are told what Leviathan is – a fleeing serpent, a twisted serpent, a dragon that lives in the sea. Let's take a look at each of these a bit more closely to gain a greater insight into the workings of this spirit.

A FLEEING SERPENT

Isaiah 27:1 refers to Leviathan as a *fleeing* serpent. At first glance this English translation might be a bit misleading – indicating that Leviathan is retreating or on the run. Leviathan will certainly retreat from the Lord Almighty when He comes at it with His great and mighty sword. We will delve into this more in the section sharing about the Strategic Keys to Overcoming Leviathan, but for now let's glean more from this Scripture about what Leviathan is and how it works.

I believe the Hebrew word *bariyach* that is translated into English here as "fleeing" has more to do with the side-to-side, darting movement of the serpent, as opposed to the concept of retreating. The NIV translates *bariyach* as "gliding." The NLT as "swiftly moving." The KJV and NKJV as "piercing." It appears that what the Lord is showing us here is that Leviathan darts from side to side in a conversation (whether it be verbal, emails, texts, etc.) to create misunderstanding and misinterpretation on both parts, causing one side to lash out at the other in an escalating war of offenses, accusations, hurt feelings, and embittered reactions. The sobering revelation to remember here is that Leviathan darts "from side to side." It is often easy to see how Leviathan is at work in someone else's midst when we're feeling misunderstood, misheard, falsely accused, or unfairly treated. But guard your heart and your words, because if you see Leviathan at work on one side of a conversation, there is an excellent chance it is at work on your side, as well. If you are feeling misunderstood, like your words are being unfairly twisted or misinterpreted, then more than likely the other person is feeling the same. Remember, Leviathan darts back and forth, doing all it can to stir up chaos and confusion on both sides.

As one of the leaders in our ministry, part of my role is pastoral – helping our team process through any conflicts that might come up by using the Kingdom values we have all committed to. It requires a willingness of everyone involved to set aside anger and offense, consider other people's perspectives, and take responsibility for any missteps or mistakes of their own that may have hurt others. I have seen this process bring forth incredible fruit again and again in my life and in our team. Because of this, there are times I am asked by other ministries to come in and help them process through their challenges and conflicts.

Not too long ago I was helping a ministry that was under a heavy attack by the spirit of Leviathan. Misunderstandings, disagreements, and accusations were breaking out amongst their usually loving team every few days. Over the course of several weeks, I found myself meeting with one person after another to hear about how they felt they had been mistreated, misrepresented, attacked, or wronged by someone. In many of the cases, there was one person who seemed to always be on the other side of the conflicts. I was able to help most of the team process through their hurts and offenses, take responsibility for any of the wrong actions on their part, and see the other party with the eyes and heart of Jesus so as to be able to truly forgive and love again. But when I met with the person who had been on the other side of so many of these conflicts, he simply was not able to see himself as part of the problem. He only saw how he had been wronged and was not able to look at how he may have misunderstood, thought wrongly about, or behaved in an unloving and ungodly manner toward all those who felt wronged by him. All he could see and talk about was how unfairly he felt he had been treated by others – sometimes getting so upset I would have to ask him to take a breath and please calm down so we could talk things through. While there had been some legitimate misunderstanding and mistreatment toward him, he was completely blind to the fact that others felt seriously mistreated by him. This person was locked up in feeling wronged and misunderstood, rationalizing and justifying his ungodly behavior, and completely unable to see that Leviathan was at work on *both* sides of all the conflicts he had been in the midst of.

First Peter 5:8 warns us to be on the alert against the enemy who prowls in our midst searching for anyone he can destroy. Leviathan is moving to and fro, looking for every opportunity to twist communications and create offenses, hurt feelings, and bitter words. This spirit works on both sides of a conflict, wanting to "pierce" relationship, poke holes in unity, and deflate cooperation so that we stop loving one another, honoring each other, and working together to advance the Kingdom.

A TWISTED SERPENT

The Hebrew word used for "serpent" here is *nachash*. It means "a snake (from its hiss)" and is derived from a root word meaning "to whisper a spell." It is the same word used in Genesis 3:1 when the enemy comes as a serpent to whisper lies to Eve and tempt her and Adam to doubt God and break relationship with Him. In John 8:44 Jesus tells us that the devil is a liar and the father of lies, and that lies are the devil's native tongue. That is still true today. The devil is a liar, and his minions are as well – including Leviathan, a

The Leviathan spirit works on both sides of a conflict, wanting to "pierce" relationship, poke holes in unity, and deflate cooperation so that we stop loving one another, honoring each other, and working together to advance the Kingdom.

spirit that hisses lies, half truths, and miscommunications into the ears of people to create misunderstanding and offense.

Isaiah 27:1 stipulates that Leviathan is not merely a "serpent," but a "twisted" serpent. That word "twisted" in Hebrew is *aqallathown*. It means "torturous," and it comes from a root word meaning "wrong." Leviathan whispers wrong interpretations of what is being communicated to trigger offense and "torture" people with hurt feelings, bitterness, and resentment so as to stir up anger, arguments, and overreactions. Leviathan works to bring chaos and confusion into communications in an attempt to turn people against one another, with the ultimate goal of damaging or breaking relationship. Leviathan wants to create division because it knows that when we are united (with God and with one another) we are unbeatable.

Psalm 133 promises that when believers are in unity, the anointing flows and God commands His blessing in our midst. What is the greatest blessing He has given us? Relationship with Him through the finished work of the Cross where every work of the enemy was overcome (1 John 3:8; John 19:30). When believers stand together in God, with God, and for God, we are "more than conquerors" (Romans 8:37), and we cannot be defeated. That is why Leviathan, the twisted serpent, whispers lies and sows half-truths into conversations, emails, texts, Facebook posts, tweets, and any other form of communication to distort, manipulate, and misrepresent what is being shared with the aim of turning brother against brother, sister against sister, husband against wife, friend against friend, parishioner against pastor, and so on. Leviathan wants us to turn on one another, snipe at one another, hiss and bite at one another. Leviathan wants to twist us into using the supernatural power of our tongues for evil instead of good, death instead of life, cursing instead of blessing (Proverbs 18:21; James 3:10).

A tell-tale sign that Leviathan is in your midst is when you find yourself in a situation where someone is upset with you and claiming, "You said *such-and-such*! You told me *this-and-that*!" And even though you try to assure them that you never said any such thing, they vehemently claim something like, "You did! I heard you say it!" Well you may not have ever spoken those exact words, but they probably did hear it, because Leviathan was twisting what you said and whispering distorted interpretations into their hearts and minds.

Let me give you an example. My wife is lovely, and I often tell her how beautiful she is. She is very gracious in receiving my compliments and usually responds with something like, "Thank you, honey." That is our normal communication. But, what if I were to say, "Baby, you look lovely today," and she responded with something like, "Are you saying that most days I look awful? Are you telling me you are no longer attracted to me? I can't believe you! That is so hurtful!"? Well, let's just say that an interaction like that would be a huge red flag alerting me that the spirit of Leviathan was in our midst, twisting communication and hissing distortions and lies in an attempt to drive a wedge between my wife and me.

A Dragon that Lives in the Sea

According to Isaiah 27:1, Leviathan is not only a serpent, it is also a dragon. A dragon that lives in the sea. This has a real depth of meaning and impact when we think of the old expression "the sea of humanity." This spirit lives in our "humanity" or "humanness" – our old carnal nature that we are supposed to be dead to, but all too often choose to "associate" with and live from, instead of our born-again divine nature.

Let's take a minute here to discuss "humanism." Humanism is one of the greatest threats to the world and church today. It is a "movement" (actually a driving spirit) that encourages people to live according to what feels right or seems right in any given situation at any given time. It exalts our humanity (the desires of our flesh and feelings) above our divine nature. It drives people to decide for themselves what is right or wrong according to what they think or feel or want, as opposed to what our wise, righteous and loving God has outlined in His Word. For example, humanism would say that sexual relations outside of marriage are fine just because we feel attraction to someone and want to sleep with them. It "makes sense" and "seems right" to our flesh, so we choose to do so even though it goes directly against the goodness of God's will and Word – not because He is a buzzkill or control freak who doesn't want us to have any fun, but because He is a loving Father who wants to protect us and others from hurt and harm.

God warns us against the traps of humanism in Isaiah 5:20 (KJV) where it says, "Woe unto them that call evil good, and good evil; that put darkness for light, and light for darkness." In Proverbs 3:5-6, He gives the wise counsel that we are not to lean on our own understanding (make our own choices of what is right and wrong), but trust in the Lord with all our hearts and submit to Him in all our ways. The reason why is shown in Proverbs 14:12 and 16:25 (NKJV): "There is a way that seems right to a man, but its end is the way of death."

In the New Testament, Jesus addresses this in Matthew 24:10-12, where He says that a day will come when many will turn away from faith in God and His Word, choosing wickedness over righteousness, growing cold toward the Lord. We certainly seem to be in that day, a day when humanism is running rampant. Humanism chooses Barabbas over Jesus (Matthew 27:21-22) – it chooses to loose the wickedness of the flesh over the righteousness of the Spirit. And Leviathan plays a part in that it works to twist our thinking, understanding, and decisions so that we make wrong choices but feel justified in them. Like when we choose to react to misunderstanding and miscommunication with irritation, offense, or frustration instead of with love and patience. It makes sense in the depth of our humanity (that sea of "self" that Leviathan lives in) to be frustrated and irritated since, after all, it is a frustrating and irritating situation to be misunderstood and accused of saying things you didn't say or mean. Our born-again nature wants us to rise above the irritation and frustration of the situation, but Leviathan wants to drag us down into the carnal depths of our humanity so we swim in the foul waters of "self," polluting everything around us.

The word "dragon" in Isaiah 27:1 is the Hebrew *taaniyn* from the root *tan* which means "to elongate." When something is elongated, it is stretched to the point of being misshapen. That is exactly what this spirit does in communication; it takes what a person says and "misshapes" it so what is heard is not what was meant – very much like that old game "telephone" in which a group sits in a circle and someone whispers a statement in the ear of the person next to them. That person then repeats it by whispering it to the person on their other side, and so on and so on, all the way around the circle. By the time the statement comes back to the person who first spoke it, it has little or nothing to do with what was originally said. The statement becomes "misshapen" due to misinterpretation and misunderstanding that gets more and more exaggerated the further it goes around the circle.

That Hebrew word *tan* – that "dragon" is derived from – can also be translated as "jackal." At first I found this confusing. After all, "to elongate" and "jackal" seemed to have nothing to do with one another. One is a verb, the other a noun. But I could feel Holy Spirit hovering and nudging me to dig deeper. So I did a little research on jackals, and found out something very interesting about them – their diet. It is referred to as an "opportunistic diet" made up mostly of small animals (rodents, ground birds, eggs) and carrion (decaying flesh of dead animals). So the root word *tan* not only gives us insight into what Leviathan does ("elongates" or misshapes communication), but also what it thrives on – the little things and our old, fleshly nature that we are supposed to be dead to. This dragon, Leviathan, takes every opportunity to feed on even the smallest of misunderstandings and stir up hurt feelings, offenses, and bitterness. It is nourished by our flesh nature that is so willing to take up offense when it feels misunderstood, then lash out, continuing the cycle until relationship and unity are destroyed. *families*

Think of the dragon in Revelation 12. It wants to devour the woman who is clothed in light wearing a crown, who is about to give birth (vv. 2, 4). The dragon persecutes the woman by opening its mouth and releasing a flood (vv. 13, 15). That crowned, pregnant woman who is clothed in light is a picture of the Bride of Christ the King, the triumphant Church, about to birth His promises in the earth. The dragon of Revelation 12 wants to destroy the woman so that she is unable to give birth to "Immanuel." Each of us is called to know the Lord intimately, and from that place of fully being His, give birth to "God in our midst" – first in our own lives, and then through our lives into the world around us, by manifesting and bearing witness of His character, nature, love, light, and life. Colossians 1:15 and Hebrews 1:3 make it clear that during Jesus' time in the earth, He was the perfect, visible, touchable, tangible representation of the reality of God. He has called us to do the works that He did (John 14:12), but we are not able to share the fullness of God with others if we are caught up in bitterness, offense, and division. The dragon Leviathan may not be perched to physically devour us, but it does devour our opportunities to share the reality of God and His Kingdom with those around us when we allow it to catch us up in our old carnal nature, as opposed to choosing to walk in the shining light of our divine, born-again nature that gives powerful witness of Jesus.

The dragon in Revelation 12 refers to Satan, but Leviathan is a minion of Satan and serves his dark master's hateful purposes with similar tactics – the main one being the "flood" that comes from its "mouth" – the torrent of misunderstandings and twisted communications it releases to create hurt feelings, anger, and offense all unto broken relationship.

KING OVER THE SONS OF PRIDE

Let's move on from Isaiah 27:1 to look at another Scripture. This is what Job 41:34 says about Leviathan:

He is king over all the sons of pride.

We learn two things here. First, that Leviathan is a king; not just some low-level demon or spirit, but a major principality. The other thing we discover is that this spirit rules and reigns over people who are "of pride." Every king has a domain (the word "kingdom," the place where a king has rule, is a shortened compound of "king's domain"). We give place to Leviathan, and invite it to rule and reign, when we enter into pride.

Pride is all about selfishness. Valuing and preferring ourselves, our agendas, our perspectives over anything or anyone else. Pride is easily offended ("How dare he say that!"). Pride is easily irritated ("That's not what I said!"). Pride is easily embittered ("I am never speaking to her again!"). Pride has no problem breaking up relationship based on misunderstanding.

When we are in pride we are way more concerned with ourselves than with others. We are caught up in our "self." Think back to what we learned in the last section, about how Leviathan "lives" in the sea of our humanness, our old carnal nature. Because of this, oftentimes when Leviathan is at work we may not even be aware of it. It just feels like "us" – our thoughts, our feelings, our reactions. But we are actually allowing Leviathan to rule and reign in us, and twist our thinking and feelings into offense, bitterness, and over-reaction. Most relationships are damaged or destroyed because one or both parties allow themselves to be trapped in a perspective of "I'm RIGHT!" This is pride – which gives place (domain) and rule (dominion) to Leviathan, the king over the sons of pride.

Because Leviathan is a king, it desires to rule. But on its own it has no actual authority. Jesus defeated it – and all the works of the enemy – at the Cross. It wants to hijack your authority as a king and steward here in the earth, and use it to achieve its wicked ends.

Perhaps you didn't realize you were a king? If you are in Christ, you are a king. Revelation 1:6 declares that you are a king and a priest. First Timothy 6:15 refers to the Lord as the King of kings. That means that He is the uppercase-K King and we are his lowercase-k kings using our God-given authority in the earth to achieve His purposes as His stewards (Genesis 1:26, Matthew 28:18-19, 1 Peter 4:10). Just as He empowered His disciples in the day of the Gospels to go forth and advance His Kingdom in the earth (Matthew 10:1, 5-8; Luke 10:1; John 17:18-20), so are we – His modern-day disciples – empowered.

Leviathan is very aware that every Christian is a king (often-times more aware than many Christians are). It knows we have authority in Christ in the earth. And it works to usurp it.

Think of the serpent in the Garden before the Fall. It knew it had no authority over Adam and Eve because they belonged to the Lord. But it also knew that if it could deceive them into using the authority they had in the earth through their relationship with God to defy Him and go against His will and ways, then he could usurp that authority and use it for his wicked agenda. The Spirit of Leviathan works just like that today. The Lord has empowered us through restored relationship and the gift of His Holy Spirit to do the works that Jesus did when He was in the earth (John 20:21-22, John 14:12). Those works include speaking words that are spirit and life, that create and have impact, that bless, edify, and encourage (John 6:63, Job 22:28, Esther 8:8, 1 Corinthians 14:3). Leviathan darts to and fro searching for believers it can deceive, tempt, or trick into using their authority in Christ to tear others down instead of building them up, to damage relationship instead of strengthening it.

A Special Warning for Leaders

Because Leviathan wants to usurp authority, the greater sphere of influence you have been entrusted with, the more likely you will be targeted by this spirit. Leaders in ministry, government, business, media, families, churches – any leaders or persons of authority – need to be especially wary and watchful for Leviathan in their midst. Have a good prayer shield established (if you do not know how to do this, we offer an excellent teaching set and manual called *The Prayer Shield* that will help you and your intercessors create a fortress of prayer around you and the assignments you are called to).

I know of one very anointed couple who started a church in British Columbia several years ago. They were influential apostolic and prophetic voices. God blessed them with favor, wisdom, and a strong building anointing. Their church grew and grew. It was a blessing to its congregants, its community, and to the world, as many missionaries and itinerant ministers were raised up through this fellowship and launched out to the nations. When the church seemed destined for even greater global impact and influence, a Leviathan spirit got in and started creating chaos and confusion in communications. Negative chatter and gossip started, murmuring and complaining were rampant – all about the lead pastors. They had meeting after meeting with individuals and groups of people to try to sort out what the issues were and how they could be constructively addressed. But every meeting seemed to only create more confusion, make matters worse, and stir up more offense, bitterness, and backbiting. After a few years of this, the church board rallied as many people as they could against the lead pastors and had them fired from their own church, the church they themselves started. Within a short time, the church was a shell of its former self – only a few people left in the congregation and little or no influence or impact locally, regionally, or globally.

All along the way the lead pastors wondered what was happening. The more they tried to hear everyone and to share their hearts with all involved, the more they were misunderstood and mistreated. It made no sense. It never does when Leviathan is involved, because when that spirit gets in, it has nothing to do with natural thinking or understanding. It is a spirit that takes what you say (and what is being said to you) and twists it around so that what is heard is radically different than what is being said.

The good news is that during this painful and difficult time, the couple pressed into the Lord, walked closely with Him, and used many of the keys that we will discuss in the section on how to overcome the spirit of Leviathan. In the end, the Lord led them into complete victory and they were restored to even greater heights.

CURSES ROUSE LEVIATHAN

Leviathan not only twists words, it can actually be drawn and empowered by them. Look at this passage in Job:

Let those who are experts at cursing, those who are ready to rouse Leviathan, curse that day.

—Job 3:8 (NLT)

Those who are "experts" at cursing (i.e., those who do it often) are rousing Leviathan – waking and drawing the spirit into their midst. The section of Scripture this comes from is when Job is going through a very difficult time. He has entered a season of tests and trials. He is in a battle. And he is none too happy about it. He allows himself to dip into discouragement and depression, and he begins to murmur and complain, cursing his own life.

Jesus said that in this life there will be trials and sorrows (John 16:33 NLT). But He bookends that statement with declarations that we may have peace in Him, and that we can take heart in any circumstance because He has overcome them all on our behalf. God does not raise up victims, He raises up victors. As part of this, there are times when He blesses us with battles so that He can train us to war and strengthen us in our faith (2 Samuel 22:35, Psalm 18:34, Psalm 144:1). Before the Lord had David take down Goliath, He mentored him in battle with first a lion and then a bear (1 Samuel 17:37). God allowed these challenges in David's life to help him get ready for what He knew was coming. It was not persecution. It was preparation. We don't become great champions by avoiding battles, but rather by embracing them and allowing the Lord to teach us how to lay hold of victory in every situation we face (2 Corinthians 2:14).

When David went into his battle against Goliath, he did so proclaiming who his God was and the victory he knew he would see (1 Samuel 17:45-47). He did not murmur. He did not complain. He did not curse his circumstances. Neither did he curse

We don't become great champions by avoiding battles, but rather by embracing them and allowing the Lord to teach us how to lay hold of victory in every situation we face.

those around him who were cowering on the sidelines. He watched over his words. And we must also. If we begin to "curse" – speak negatively about our situation, others, ourself, or God – we will rouse Leviathan, drawing and empowering this spirit. This creates even more chaos or confusion and exacerbates the challenges we are facing. Instead of having people drawn to us who will be a blessing, we will have "friends" like Job's, coming and giving twisted counsel that works to draw us into greater self-pity, confusion, and despair.

As we have seen, Leviathan works to create chaos in communication, twisting how things are heard to cause misunderstanding and offense. It wants to set people against one another, turning comrades into critics and allies into accusers. Its desire is that in the midst of the confusion we will start to speak badly about one another, cursing each other. This empowers the spirit to wreak even more havoc and bring even more destruction.

BE CAREFUL WHAT YOU "EAT" IN THE DESERT

Psalm 74:14 is yet another Leviathan scripture; in it there is a revelation about how this spirit can take advantage of challenging seasons in our life. Here is what it says:

You crushed the heads of Leviathan and let the desert animals eat him.
—Psalm 74:14 (NLT)

Take note that I am using the New Living Translation (NLT) of the above Scripture. The NLT is what I tend to use for my daily prayer and devotional times with the Lord. The NLT translates Psalm 74:14 a bit differently than most other translations. Where it says, "and let the desert animals eat him," most other Bible versions read like the NASB (one of my other favorite translations), saying something along the lines of: "You gave him as food for the creatures of the wilderness." The NASB translation makes it clear that the Lord has crushed Leviathan, and then gave the defeated foe to the dwellers in the desert as food. What a powerful illustration that what the enemy means for harm, God turns to good (Genesis 50:20). When we walk with God, the giants that come against us in the desert can become our "food" to fuel us on the journey into the Promised Land!

In addition to the powerful revelation we receive from the NASB and similar translations, I would like to dig into the NLT version of this Scripture and take a bit of license to make a different application. Sometimes the Spirit will speak *rhema* revelation from a Scripture that is out of context but it will be congruent with the full counsel of God. I believe there is something additional the Lord would have us see in the wording of the NLT where it says, "and let the desert animals eat him"– a very pertinent warning to watch what we choose to "eat" when we are in the "desert."

The desert is a picture of the dry, difficult seasons of our lives. Times when we have not yet seen the manifestation of God's promises, when we are in transition and often in confusion about what is going on and why. When we are in the desert, it is important that we "eat" the right "food," and that we commune at the right "table." The Lord Almighty has crushed the head of Leviathan, every work of the enemy has been defeated at the Cross (Colossians 2:15, 1 John 3:8, John 19:30). But even so, if during difficult times we in our own free will choose to "eat" of Leviathan, the Lord will let us. He loves us so much that He will never violate our free will, even if we make bad choices in it.

During desert times, we are meant to "eat" of God. He will supply all our needs, at all times, in all situations – if we choose to turn to Him and trust in Him. Just as He gave manna to His people in the literal desert of Sinai, He will give each of us the true manna of His life, love, light, presence, power, and provision in any figurative desert of difficult circumstances we find ourselves in (John 6:32-33). We are to eat of Him, sup with Him, and commune with Him during these challenging seasons. Psalm 23:5 makes it clear that there is great blessing for us when we do. It states that He has prepared a "feast" for us in the presence of our enemies. During the difficult times when the enemy seems to have us surrounded, God is not only right there with us but, if we choose to turn to Him and trust Him as our source in those moments, He has an abundance of good things for us! He will welcome us during these times, anoint us afresh with His presence, and pour out upon us until our cup is overflowing with blessings!

Leviathan knows all of this. That is why when we are in the "desert," it works to get us to eat of him as opposed to the manna of God. It wants us to partake of his confusion, chaos, and misunderstandings so that instead of choosing to receive fresh counsel, wisdom, knowledge, patience, and love from the Lord (what a feast!), we will choose to receive offense, bitterness, anger, hurt feelings, and irritation from the enemy.

Be careful whose table you sit at during your desert times!

LEVIATHAN AND DISEASE

*For if you eat the bread or drink the cup unworthily, **not honoring the body of Christ,** you are eating and drinking God's judgment upon yourself. **That is why many of you are weak and sick and some have even died.***

—*1 Corinthians 11:29-30 (NLT)*

Even though this passage of 1 Corinthians is not directly about Leviathan, in it we find a profound revelation that shows one of the subtlest and most hidden ways this snake attacks and wreaks havoc.

In the United States alone there are tens of millions of people who are suffering with autoimmune diseases, degenerative condi- *Allergies* tions, and genetic disorders. Globally I am sure those numbers would be multiplied several times. Of course there are many root causes of illness, and not every one of these cases is an assault of the spirit of Leviathan, but I invite you to consider the following insight I received from the Lord. This revelation is another weapon in our spiritual arsenal against sickness and disease.

In previous Scriptures we have seen that Leviathan twists communication to set one person against another. That is how it attacks "externally" between individuals, but I believe that there is a clue here in 1 Corinthians 11 about how Leviathan can also attack "internally" within an individual, creating sickness and disease.

In 1 Corinthians 11:17-30, the apostle Paul speaks to the church at Corinth about issues among them that are creating division (1 Corinthians 11:18). He starts out by saying that "it sounds as if more harm than good is done when you meet together" (1 Corinthians 11:17). Doesn't that sound like Leviathan? People come together to discuss an issue, but in the conversation more harm than good is done until ultimately there is division?

The issue on the surface that is being discussed by the church at Corinth has to do with communion. But they are not finding agreement, unity, and understanding. Instead they are taking offense, sniping at each other, and turning against one another.

All this disagreement and dishonor among the believers is causing disease in the church – many are "weak and sick and some
have even died" (1 Corinthians 11:30). I believe Holy Spirit is giving us a clue here that when Leviathan is in our midst, it not only
can cause disagreement and disharmony between believers, but
it also can cause disagreement and disharmony within a believer.

Sickness and disease can occur when the body and its systems no longer function optimally due to confusion, chaos, or
internal miscommunication. Think of autoimmune disorders like
lupus, Hashimoto's disease, rheumatoid arthritis, Addison's disease, Type 1 diabetes. These all occur when the immune system
– created to defend the body from disease – becomes confused
and begins attacking the body, harming the very systems, organs,
glands, and tissues it is meant to protect and heal. Similarly, degenerative conditions and genetic disorders like Parkinson's, ALS,
cerebral palsy, muscular dystrophy and cystic fibrosis are caused
because there is major miscommunication between the brain
or central nervous system and the other systems or cells of the
body. Miscommunication and confusion resulting in damage and
destruction – that is evidence of the twisting serpent Leviathan.

If you – or a precious one you know – are overcoming such a
condition, consider seeking the guidance of the Lord in praying
and binding the works of Leviathan in your midst.

3

STRATEGIC KEYS TO OVERCOMING LEVIATHAN

I n the previous section we examined scriptural insights into what the spirit of Leviathan is, how it works, and ways that it manifests. We learned that it is a major demonic power causing serious problems in the church and for believers. It is wise to be aware of this spirit and its workings, but realize that you don't need to be afraid of it. Remember that the spirit of Leviathan, along with every other demonic power, was defeated at the Cross of Calvary by the Lord. When Jesus declared, "It is finished" (John 19:30), He was announcing for all time that He had triumphed over every manifestation of hell and death. Including Leviathan!

In this section, you will learn how to lay hold of that victory and prevail against Leviathan wherever and whenever it manifests. God has revealed powerful keys for overcoming this spirit. Each is a strategic tool that will help you see the works of Leviathan dismantled and rendered naught when you discover it moving in your midst.

Key One:

HUMILITY

Whenever I think of humility, I think of the great quote attributed to C.S. Lewis – "Humility is not thinking less of yourself, it is thinking of yourself less." True humility, or "going low" as it is sometimes referred to, takes "self" out of the equation.

In the world, it is all about self. What do I get? How will I be seen? How am I being treated? What's in it for me? When, where, how, and how often, do I get mine? The I-Me-Mine motivation of self-interest, self-promotion, and self-protection – in other words, selfishness.

But in the Kingdom it is different. Think of Jesus in John 13. In this passage of Scripture it says that Jesus knew where He had come from and where He was going, so He took off His robe, wrapped a towel around His waist, poured water into a basin, and began to wash the disciples' feet (John 13:3-5). What a picture of humility. The Lord Himself, not demanding to be served but instead being a servant to all. The key for us to see here is in the first part of the passage where it says Jesus knew where He had come from and where He was going (v. 3). Jesus was so secure in the goodness, wisdom, plan, purpose, might, and ability of the Heavenly Father that He knew He did not need to have His mind on Himself. He knew that the Father so cared for Him and had Him so covered in all things at all times, He was free to give Himself away. He did not need to be watching out for Himself, because He knew how completely His Father was watching over Him.

It is the same for each of us in the Kingdom. We can be certain of the goodness of our God, and rest in that. Think about this: Not only does Jesus love and care for us here in the earth as the Father loved and cared for Him (John 15:9), but because of Jesus, the Father now loves us as much as He loves Jesus (John 17:22-23). Amazing! Knowing that we belong to someone who loves and cares for us so completely and perfectly that He gave everything for us, and also gave everything to us (Romans 8:32), can free the Body of Christ from self and selfishness as much as it did Jesus when He was in the earth.

Because we are our Beloved's and He is ours (Song of Songs 6:3), we no longer need to be concerned with how we are (or aren't) being treated, received, or spoken about. We can be certain that God loves us and plans to bless, prosper, and do good things for us (Jeremiah 29:11), AND that He is well able to bring forth all of these good plans despite any resistance of the enemy, or how things might look or feel at any given moment (Genesis 28:15, 2 Corinthians 2:14). This all gives us the ability to let go of self and go low, even in the most challenging or unfair circumstances – which works to significantly disempower the spirit of Leviathan.

Remember what we learned from Job 41:34 – Leviathan rules over the "sons of pride." When this spirit is active we can easily get caught up in our "self," our human-ness, and pride. We will find ourselves thinking things like, "I'm right!" "I can't believe they said that!" "That's not fair!" "How dare they!" We find ourselves reacting and overreacting, becoming defensive, lashing out, tak-ing offense, building cases against others, gossiping, and working to get those around us to take up offenses on our behalf. All of which are huge indications that Leviathan is active, and that it is time to go low and embrace humility!

Choosing humility connects us to the power and victory of the Cross. Jesus did not hold our wrongs against us – just the opposite. He forgave our wrongs and chose to serve us even when we were maligning Him, speaking ill of Him, lying about Him, treating Him unfairly, and persecuting Him. When we go low and embrace humility, instead of being offended by what others did to us, we start taking responsibility for how we are responding. Pride rationalizes and justifies wrong responses. Humility embraces righteousness. Humility understands that it is not about being right, it is about responding in a right way – breaking the cycle of pride, misunderstanding, offense, gossip, and retaliation that the spirit of Leviathan fuels and is fueled by.

I have mentioned gossip a few times in this section. It is one of the manifestations of pride. Pride wants to be right, so when we are mistreated our pride wants to tell everyone who is willing to listen – sharing all the details of how unfairly we have been treated – in an effort to get them to "take our side" against the person who wronged us. It may make our flesh feel better in the moment, but in the long run it only adds fuel to Leviathan's fire and makes matters worse. What usually happens is that the people we "vent" to take up our offense. They then tell others, who then go and tell even more people. And so on. All the while the whole thing gets even more twisted and blown out of proportion along the way (remember that Leviathan rules over the sons of pride and twists communications to create chaos and confusion with the goal of damaging or destroying relationships).

When it comes to gossip, the best approach is to not speak it or spread it. A good rule of thumb is to never say anything about a person that you would not say if they were sitting right there with you. And as far as listening to gossip, don't! Leviathan is at work in gossip, you can't trust what you hear. It is rife with misunderstanding.

Leviathan was defeated at the Cross. So as soon as we become aware that it is in our midst, it is important for us to embrace the Cross through humility. When we put on the "brown cloak" of humility we walk as Jesus did, a servant to all. We care about others, treat them fairly, and are honoring toward them, regardless of how they treat us. That is what true humility looks like. We go low, refuse offense, forgive those who have wronged us, and choose to only speak well of others. This disempowers Leviathan by giving it nothing to work with.

Choosing humility connects us to the power and victory of the Cross. Jesus did not hold our wrongs against us – just the opposite. He forgave our wrongs and chose to serve us even when we were maligning Him.

Key Two:

REPENTANCE

In John 14:30 Jesus says, "The ruler of the world is coming, and he has nothing in Me." Jesus gave no place – in His heart, thoughts, or words – to Satan or any of his minions. Neither should we. Yet all too often we do, usually without even realizing it.

As we discussed in the previous section on Humility, Leviathan reigns over those who are in pride (Job 41:34). Pride plays a huge part in most arguments and disagreements. We are so sure we are right – or that we have been wronged – we refuse to consider the other person's points or perspectives. We demand to be heard, but are not willing to listen. When we give in to pride like this, we give place to Leviathan. We empower the twisted serpent to hiss its lies into our ears and hearts. But fear not. For where the Spirit of the Lord is, there is freedom (2 Corinthians 3:17) – including freedom from pride!

When Leviathan is in our midst, it is critical that we ask Holy Spirit to search our hearts and reveal anything in us that is in agreement with pride, or anything else that would give place to the manipulations of this demonic king. Invite Holy Spirit to go deep, and be open to His loving conviction and correction. Know that He is not revealing things to you to make you feel guilty or ashamed, but to set you free and empower you.

The enemy will try to get you to hold on to pride, bitterness, offense, and the like. It will work to justify negativity, murmuring, complaining, gossip, and speaking ill of others. It will try to convince you that these are legitimate responses and appropriate reactions to the unfair things that have been said about you or done to you. But each of them is a trap. And all of them give place to Leviathan. Repent of whatever Holy Spirit shows you. Plead the blood of Jesus over the words, attitudes, and behaviors that He reveals have given place to Leviathan in your midst. Receive the forgiveness of the Cross; thank the Lord that He has made you brand new in body, soul, and spirit (2 Corinthians 5:17); and rejoice that the thief has been caught, must pay back sevenfold, and that now you are able to ransack *his* house (Proverbs 6:31).

Repentance removes from our hearts and lives things that are "landing strips" for the enemy. When you have nothing in agreement with Leviathan, it still can come but will have no place in you. This allows you to use the keys in this section to disempower it and nullify its influences in your life.

Before we move on, allow me to point out another wonderful benefit of repentance. Acts 3:19-20 shows us that not only are our sins forgiven and landing strips for the enemy removed when we repent, but it also opens a door in the spirit so that "times of refreshing may come from the presence of the Lord." When we repent, it draws the presence of the Lord and He refreshes us from the wounds and weariness of our battles with Leviathan. So repent ... and be refreshed!

Key Three:

LOVE

In a battle, usually the side with the biggest, best and most powerful weapons wins. Well, there is no greater weapon than love – *love never fails* (1 Corinthians 13:8).

God is love (1 John 4:8). When we are beset by the enemy but choose the divine response of love instead of a myriad of selfish or carnal responses, we invite God into the fray. When we choose love, it opens the door for the Lord Almighty, the Lord invincible in battle (Psalm 24:8) to come in and bring forth the victory (2 Corinthians 2:14).

It is important that we clearly see just how powerful love is; how total and complete the victory over the enemy is when we choose love no matter what. Think of Jesus. It was love that brought Him into the earth on man's behalf (John 3:16). When man did not receive Jesus or make a place for Him (Luke 2:7), He chose love and came anyway. When man brutally slaughtered every male child two years of age and younger in and around Bethlehem in an attempt to murder Jesus as a baby (Matthew 2:16), He did not give up on us but instead chose to love us still. When He began His earthly ministry and helped, blessed, healed, and delivered everyone He encountered (Acts 10:38); man responded by speaking poorly of Him, calling Him demon-possessed (John 7:20), a lunatic (John 10:20), a criminal (John 18:30), a heretic and blasphemer (Matthew 26:65), and driving Him from our midst (Luke 8:37). Jesus did not take offense or leave us to ourselves. He chose love. When one of those closest to Him betrayed Him with a kiss, He did not lash back, but instead called him "friend" (Matthew 26:50), refusing to withdraw love no matter how He was treated. When one of His most trusted denied Him three times, swearing by God that he did not know Him (Matthew 26:74); Jesus chose love, turning His face to him (Luke 22:61), making sure that he knew that even if he withdrew love from Jesus, Jesus would never withdraw love from him. When man flogged Him, whipped Him, beat Him, spit on Him, mocked Him, and called for His death (Mark 15:15, 19; Luke 23:21), Jesus' response was to continue to love. When man hung Him on the cross, ridiculing Him, shouting abuses and hurling taunts (Matthew 27:35-41), Jesus' response was not to shout back but instead choose love, beseeching heaven on our behalf, "Father, forgive them; for they know not what they do" (Luke 23:34 KJV). Jesus chose love every step of the way. He refused not to love. No matter what. In every circumstance and situation. The end result was that all of hell and death were defeated (Revelation 1:18, Matthew 28:18, 1 John 3:8). That is the power of love – complete, utter, and total victory over the enemy, his minions and manifestations. That is the power that you bring to the battle when, regardless of how you are treated, you choose to love.

Leviathan works in direct opposition to love. It creates misunderstanding, bitterness, and offense in an attempt to drive people apart and destroy relationship. This is why love is such a powerful key to seeing this spirit overcome. When we choose love, we choose to move in the opposite spirit of Leviathan. We choose to value people and invest in relationship instead of exalting and protecting pride and selfishness.

First Corinthians 13:4-7 outlines for us what love looks like, how it behaves, and the choices it makes. Let's take some of the key passages from those verses and unpack them one at a time to give us a better understanding of how the "super-weapon" of love overcomes the spirit of Leviathan.

Love Is Patient *(v. 4)*

Leviathan wants us to have a hair trigger, quickly responding angrily to every slight by lashing out in an ever-escalating war of over-reaction. Love, however, is patient – able to accept and allow imperfections and challenges without becoming annoyed or reactive.

Love Is Kind *(v. 4 NLT)*

Leviathan works to catch us up in ourselves so that we are only concerned about how *we* are being treated or spoken about, and overreacting when we feel wronged. But love is kind, always concerned with the other person, treating them as a friend, and preferring them over "self" at all times. The kindness of love causes us to reach out instead of lash out, wanting to find a way to bless and serve the other person as opposed to defending against them or speaking ill about them.

Love Is Not Proud *(v. 4 NIV)*

Pride and selfishness are Leviathan's playground. Job 41:34 makes it clear that when we are in pride we give rule and reign to Leviathan. We saw in Key One how effective *humility* is at taking this spirit out. Love is not proud. It is humble. And when we choose love, we disempower Leviathan.

Love Does Not Dishonor Others *(v. 5 NIV)*

Leviathan stirs us up so that we speak ill of one another, but love refuses to be dishonoring. Love always finds something good to say. Think of Jesus when He first met Nathanael in John 1. Nathanael had dishonored Him by saying, "What good can come from Nazareth?" But when Jesus met Nathanael, He did not dishonor in return. Instead, He found something good to say about Nathanael (John 1:46, 47). When we refuse to speak poorly of another, it gives no place to Leviathan on our side of the communication. It can only be a fight if both sides are throwing punches.

Love Does Not Demand Its Own Way *(v. 5 NLT)*

Love is not self-seeking. It does not demand to be treated, received, or spoken about in a certain way. Leviathan wants to stir up selfishness and pride when things are not going how we want them to. It wants to provoke us to respond in bitterness and frustration. But love does not demand its own way. Love knows that the Lord is our way-maker (Isaiah 43:16) and our provider (Philippians 4:19). Love allows us to rest in Him, trusting Him for every good thing (Psalm 23:1) as opposed to demanding them from others.

Love Is Not Provoked *(v. 5)*

Remember what we learned about Leviathan in Isaiah 27:1? It is a serpent that darts from *side to side* in a conversation, creating misunderstanding on *both* sides to stir one against the other. Leviathan relies on both parties becoming increasingly provoked and lashing out. But love is not provoked. Love does not respond negatively. Love does not get angry or bitter. When we choose love, we establish an impenetrable barrier that keeps Leviathan out of our side of communications.

Love Keeps No Record of When It Has Been Wronged *(v. 5 NLT)*

One of the things that fuels offense is a history of offense. When we keep a record of having been wronged – an active, running list of all the slights, hurts, and disappointments that have happened to us over the years – we can fall into a victim mentality, dreading yet also looking for the next wrong, the next hurt. Leviathan thrives in that atmosphere – twisting the least little thing into an inner explosion of frustration and irritation that causes us to over-react in a hurt, negative way. Love lets go of wrongs and does not take offense. A powerful point to remember here is that offense can be given but it does not have to be taken. Even if someone does something offensive toward you, you have the power in love to refuse to take up an offense. You were created in love, by love, and for love to be a victor, not a victim. Do not give your power away by living in a victim mentality with a long record of hurts and wrongs that you regularly review. Cast those cares upon the Lord!

Love Looks For the Best in Each Person *(v. 7 AMP)*

Leviathan relies on you misinterpreting the words and actions of those around you. It will take the least little thing and twist it into a seeming slight, plus "help you" assign a negative motive and intent to it. In other words, Leviathan not only twists your take on what others are saying or doing, but it will also work to get you to believe the worst about them and the reason they are doing it. Leviathan wants us to think badly about the people around us.

Even if someone does something offensive toward you, you have the power in love to refuse to take up an offense. You were created in love, by love, and for love to be a victor, not a victim.

But when we choose love, we choose to believe the best about people, no matter what. If someone is short with us or ignores us, Leviathan will try to twist that and make you believe they are a bad person who does not respect you because they think they are so much more important than you. But love would choose to believe that the person is simply in a hurry – perhaps they just really need to get to the bathroom!

Several years ago someone in my workplace exploded at me one day. As I was leaving our building she chased me down and said, "I have had it with you!" I was surprised, as I had no idea what I had done to upset her so. When I shared that with her, she exploded again, "How can you not know? You have intentionally been hurting me! I am sick and tired of your arrogance and cruelty!"

Now none of us like to be accused or attacked, especially if it feels unfair. Initially my flesh wanted to rise up and shout back something like, "What are you talking about, you crazy person!" But instead, I took a breath, looked her in the eye, and said, "I am sorry you are so upset, please sit down with me and help me understand." So right there, we sat down and she shared with me how when I came into our small office building, I usually went into the front room adjacent to the offices, checked my mailbox for any work that had piled up, and then I would often "just leave."

I responded, yes, that was true, but I didn't understand how it was hurting her. She said she knew I was intentionally ignoring her each time I came into the building so as to hurt her and put her in her place. I asked what had given her that idea. Her answer was that she simply knew that was the case because I hardly ever ducked my head into her office to say hello. Even though she made it quite clear that she felt singled out, she also angrily observed that I seldom interacted with anyone in the building during office hours. She let me know that this had tormented her for months, she was done putting up with it, and it was time to let me have it.

I thanked her for being so open and honest with me, and apologized that my behavior had hurt her. Then I asked if it would be okay with her for me to share my perspective on it all. When she allowed me to speak, I shared that I can be quite task-oriented at times, but I assured her that my behavior was never meant to ignore or dishonor her in any way, and certainly I had never wanted to "torture" her. Just the opposite. To my mind, I explained, I had been honoring her (and other office workers) by not intruding upon them, interrupting their work, or breaking their concentration when I came into the building. I reminded her of several times when I had stepped into her office, or the office of others, when they were not busy, to say hello and visit a bit. We ended up talking the whole thing through. I thanked her for helping me to see her perspective, as it was a good reminder to me to get out of task-mode and engage with the people around me even when I am very busy. I also gently let her know that if anything like that came up again, she should simply come to me and talk to me about it right away rather than being tormented by it for months. She said, yes, she wished she had done that, as it would have saved her a lot of irritation and energy.

Do you see how Leviathan got in and made such a mess? Twisting in her mind the *why* of *what* I was doing? If this precious woman had simply chosen early on to believe the best about me ("oh, he is probably very busy" or "how nice that he is so respectful of our space and workload"), it would have saved her months of aggravation. It also would have allowed her to communicate early on something like, "I know you are very busy and are probably trying to respect our workspace, but we sure do like it when you take a minute to say hi when you come into the building."

If you refuse to think anything but the best about someone, the twisted lies and misinterpretations of other people's actions (and motives) that Leviathan tries to plant in your mind and heart will find no place and will simply fall away.

Love Never Loses Faith *(v. 7 NLT)*

When we are in love, we are in faith. Love never doubts that God is able – in all things, at all times – to provide for us and to bring about a good end from any circumstance or situation. Because of this, when we choose love we are free of the manipulations of Leviathan that want us to be angry with people who have failed or disappointed us. Love knows that people are not our source, so we never have to be afraid that we are not getting from them what we need, expect, or feel we deserve. Love keeps us in faith that God, not others, is our source, and that He has good things for us even if at a given moment people do not.

It is not always easy to choose love, but it is always powerful. And the more often we choose love, the easier it gets and the greater the multiplied impact. That's why we should never shy away from our "love tests." They are not a burden to be avoided, but a blessing to be embraced. I have found over the years that my greatest love tests were my greatest opportunities for increase and acceleration. I have not "passed" them all. But the ones in which I did choose love over and over again, I not only saw the enemy defeated in my midst, I also saw a greater Kingdom authority arise in me. So the next time you are being mistreated or misunderstood, don't focus on how unfair it all is; focus on the amazing fruit that will come forth from the victory of choosing to do, think, and speak like love!

Love Is Not a Doormat

Before we move on to the next Key to overcoming Leviathan, there is one other thing I would like to discuss in regards to love. We have talked quite a bit about what love is. Now let's take a minute to talk about what love is not. Love is not a doormat. Love is not passive. Love acts. Love confronts and speaks the truth, but *always* for the good of the other person – to empower them, to help them see a blind spot in their lives, or to edify them. Love does not shame, attack, or accuse. Love reminds people who they are to help set them free of the enemy's snares that have momentarily caught them up in who they are not.

We have built our ministry on a foundation of Kingdom values that are based on the character and nature of Jesus. These values are a "plumb line" that we all have committed to. Part of that commitment involves agreeing to be held accountable to those values. If I violate one of the values, someone on our team will confront me about it (although quite often Holy Spirit beats them to it). But when they do, they confront me in love. Not attacking me for where I fell short, but reminding me where I can come up higher.

This love approach to confrontation is always *for* the person, never *against* them. It is always spoken in hope and faith and love, never irritation or frustration. It does not confront to condemn or shame, but to edify and empower.

Sometimes the most loving thing we can do is to reach out to someone in the midst of a misunderstanding, sharing our hearts and listening to theirs. This approach – as opposed to attacking someone or simply "writing them off" – can take the teeth out of Leviathan's schemes and work to repair and restore relationship.

It is not always easy to choose love, but it is always powerful. And the more often we choose love, the easier it gets and the greater the multiplied impact.

Key Four:

LISTENING AND HEARING

James 1:19 tells us to be quick to listen and slow to speak. That is wise counsel when the spirit of Leviathan is active. This spirit creates misunderstanding to trigger hurt and offense. When we feel misunderstood we can be too quick to jump in, cut the other person off, and attempt to defend ourselves with more words. But Leviathan simply twists those words as well, creating even greater misunderstanding in an ever-increasing cycle of chaos, confusion, frustration and anger. When overcoming Leviathan, silence is often golden. Not a withdrawn, arms-crossed, I-give-up silence – but an open-hearted, closed-mouth silence where we are truly trying to hear what the other person is saying and where they are coming from. Often it is much more effective to simply listen, and then take the issues to the Lord. He will give us the perspective and understanding we need way beyond any words that have been spoken. He never twists meaning or understanding. He never brings confusion. He knows the heart of all people in all things. He will help you understand the root of the issues and how to best bring peaceful, healing resolution.

Often when we are in conversation (especially when there is conflict), we are not listening to the other person nearly as much as we are in our heads thinking how we can respond, what we will say when they are done talking, or looking for an opportunity to jump in and make *our* point. We want to get the next word in. We want to win. We are so concerned with being heard ourselves that we are not making an effort to hear the other person. This perpetuates or escalates the conflict as opposed to defusing it.

Good listening skills are a powerful weapon against the spirit of Leviathan. They nullify the chaos, confusion, and hyper-reactiveness the spirit works to stir up in communications. When you become aware that Leviathan is in your midst, be less concerned about making your point (the spirit will simply work to twist it anyway), and be more concerned about hearing the other person's heart. What are they really trying to say? What is behind their flurry of words and accusations? If you are not sure, let them know that you really want to understand their heart, and ask good affirming questions such as: "It sounds to me that you're saying this: ___. Is that correct?" Or, "I really want to understand your heart in this; can you tell me what you're feeling?"

When people feel they are being listened to – that an attempt is being made to hear their side of a matter – they feel valued. This alone can go a long way in de-escalating tense situations and overcoming the turmoil that Leviathan creates and thrives in.

One other thing for us to remember that will help us be good listeners: *We all know in part* (1 Corinthians 13:9). Listening helps us get beyond the sometimes limited perspective of our own established framework and opens us up to hear (and learn from) others. If we are too entrenched in our own point-of-view and too prideful to consider another's feelings or opinions on a matter, we can very quickly become narrow-minded. There is a blessing in being a good listener even beyond seeing Leviathan defeated. Being a good listener will help you be a life-long learner.

When we listen well – hearing not only the words but also the heart of another – it helps untangle the twisted communications of Leviathan. God is all about the heart, and His favorite place to meet people is exactly where they are. If we embrace this posture by partnering with Holy Spirit in our listening, it opens the door for God to give us insights and understandings that will unravel the deceptions and distortions of Leviathan.

The Keys Work Together

I want to take a minute to point out how well the Keys work together. For example, we need Humility and Love to be a good listener. When we go low and prefer the other person over ourselves, our goal in communications becomes wanting to understand the person across from us more than we want be understood. The keys of Humility, Love, and Listening work powerfully together to effectively cripple Leviathan because we refuse to believe anything but good about the other person, knowing they have as much value as we do, and our great desire is to hear them so that they feel understood. We no longer want to be right nearly so much as righteous. We no longer want to win so much as see victory come forth in the situation. No single Key on its own may totally take out Leviathan, but used together they unlock the character and nature of Jesus in us and work to untwist the effects of this scheming serpent.

Key Five:

GUARD COMMUNICATION

Proverbs 18:21 tells us that our tongue has the power of life and death. A major part of Leviathan's assault is to agitate us into speaking words of death toward one another – negative, judgmental, accusative, bitter, hateful, diminishing words spoken out of hurt, anger, and frustration. Leviathan wants us to speak death to one another as opposed to speaking life. That is why we must guard our communications and watch over our words very carefully when this spirit is active.

In John 6:26-69, Jesus is dealing with what by all appearances could very well be an attack of Leviathan. The spirit is not mentioned by name, but many of the hallmarks of its workings are seen throughout the passage. There is misunderstanding, murmuring, complaining, and disagreement (vv. 42-43); arguing amongst one another (v. 52); confusion (v. 60); offense (v. 61), and broken relationships (v. 66). Through it all, Jesus as always is very intentional about what He says and how He says it. He does not enter into argument or offense. He watches over His heart and His words, speaking only that which is spirit and life (v. 63). He doesn't take offense, He doesn't get angry, He doesn't speak out of irritation or frustration. He gives Leviathan no place in Him or His communications, and because of this He is able to overcome the enemy's ultimate goal of driving a wedge between Him and His core team (vv. 67-69).

Just as Jesus models to us, we must guard our communications in the midst of a Leviathan attack. Watch over your words. Just as importantly, watch over your heart, because from the abundance of your heart your mouth will speak (Luke 6:45). If you know your heart is not in the right place at the moment, close your mouth. Once words are out, they cannot be taken back. This is especially true with texts, emails, social media posts, blogs, and other written forms of communication. It might feel "good" to vent in the moment, but all you are really doing is pouring fuel on Leviathan's fire and giving that twisting snake more opportunities to create more misunderstanding, anger, hurt, and offense. However, if you make an effort to be mindful of your words – spoken, written, texted, posted – and are careful to only communicate that which is life and truth in love – well, that takes the teeth out of the serpent and makes it much harder for it to inject its venom into the situation.

We must guard our communications in the midst of a Leviathan attack. Watch over your words. Just as importantly, watch over your heart, because from the abundance of your heart your mouth will speak.

Key Six:

DECREES

Isaiah 27:1 declares that the Lord will punish Leviathan with His fierce, great and mighty sword. Ephesians 6:17 tells us that the Word of God is a sword. When we are in warfare, the Word is a weapon we can wield to exact vengeance against spiritual enemies, powers, and principalities.

In Genesis 1, there is a profound revelation of how great and mighty the declared Word of God is, and how effective it is in bringing forth order in the midst of confusion. There was darkness and chaos everywhere (v. 2), but when the Lord spoke – BOOM – everything shifted. He said, "Let there be light; and there was light" (v. 3). No debate, no resistance, no delay. Just BOOM. Done. That is the power we bring to bear against the spirit of Leviathan when we make faith-filled decrees of God's Word.

As we have seen, Leviathan is a snake (Isaiah 27:1), and in Luke 10:19 Jesus announced that He has given us authority over all the power of the enemy – including treading upon (crushing underfoot) snakes. The context of this passage in Luke 10 is Jesus sending out His disciples to do His works and advance the Kingdom in the earth, and to see Satan and his minions defeated (Luke 10:17-18). Part of the Lord's instructions was that everywhere the disciples went, they were to declare that the Kingdom of Heaven was at hand (v. 9). In other words, they were to make decrees! When we open our mouths to speak forth the truth and reality of the Kingdom, we tread upon and crush "snakes" – snakes such as Leviathan!

Declaring the Word of God releases eternal truth into situations that are temporarily overcome by momentary facts. Facts change. Truth does not. And the declared truth of God's Word slices through temporary circumstances, tearing down the deceptions of darkness and establishing the reality of the Kingdom (Jeremiah 1:9-10). This is especially effective against Leviathan. Our own words can be twisted and manipulated by this spirit to make matters worse. But the Word of the Lord accomplishes all it is sent to do, it never returns void, it always prospers and succeeds (Isaiah 55:11). When we proclaim His Word in faith, the Lord exalts and honors His Word (Psalm 138:2), and armies of heaven's angels are released to carry out His commands and establish His truth (Psalm 103:20). The declared Word of God is like an atomic blast in the spirit. Leviathan will not be able to hold its twisting, deceiving, manipulating ground against it.

Wielding the Word Against Leviathan

When you discover Leviathan in your midst, do not rely on your own words or your ability to untwist its deceptions and manipulations. Turn to God's Word. There is a scriptural truth for every circumstance and situation. That is the word you want to wield against the lies and misrepresentations of this spirit. Seek the Lord. When He reveals the Word to you, declare that Scripture in faith. Send forth that decree – again and again, if need be. It will succeed.

For example, the Word of God says that the Lord is "the way, and the truth" (John 14:6); that He is the "the LORD, strong and

> *When you discover Leviathan in your midst, do not rely on your own words or your ability to untwist its deceptions and manipulations. Turn to God's Word. There is a scriptural truth for every circumstance and situation.*

mighty, the LORD, invincible in battle" (Psalm 24:8); that He rescues us from every trap of the enemy (Psalm 91:3); and that He leads us into all truth (John 16:13). We can take these Scriptures, turn them into decrees, and wield them against Leviathan by declaring:

> *Jesus, I invite You into this situation. I declare that You are wielding the fierce, great, and mighty Sword of Your Word against Leviathan. Have Your way! Bring forth Your truth! King of Glory, thank You that You are coming into this battle. You are almighty. You are invincible. Leviathan is defeated in our midst. I decree that You have set me, and everyone involved in this situation, free from every trap of Leviathan that would ensnare us in misunderstanding, offense, anger, or confusion. As You lead us into all truth, I declare that deception and disagreement fall away. Thank You for shining the light of Your truth upon every one of our communications. I declare that the darkness of Leviathan's lies, misrepresentations, and manipulations are all shattered. In Your mighty name I pray, Jesus. Amen.*

Similarly, you can wield the Sword of the Spirit against Leviathan by covering yourself so that its schemes and machinations come to naught. Take Scriptures like Isaiah 54:17, Genesis 50:20, Psalm 5:12, Zechariah 2:5, Psalm 27:13, Romans16:20 and turn them into a decree that you send forth. It will go out into the spirit and slay the operation of Leviathan in your midst:

No weapon formed against me shall prosper. Every tongue that rises up against me in judgment or false accusation is refuted, confuted, and condemned. The enemy's schemes, attacks, and obfuscations are rendered null and void. Thank You, Lord, that You surround me with Your favor as a shield, and You are a glory in my midst. I am covered and protected. I will see the goodness of God in the midst of these attacks of Leviathan! Praise You, Lord, that You give me peace as the enemy is crushed beneath my feet! In Jesus' name I pray. Amen.

Wielding the Word for the Other Party

Not only can you wield the Word against Leviathan, you can also wield it on behalf of the other people involved in the situation that Leviathan has gotten in the midst of.

This spirit wants to create mistrust, offense, bitterness, and anger between people. Its goal is to drive a wedge in relationships through misunderstanding, hurt feelings, and overreaction. It wants us to turn on each other and speak poorly about one another. So a very effective weapon against this spirit is to speak blessings from the Word of God over the other people involved.

Seek the Lord for Scriptures you can decree over them that will bless them, cover them, and edify them in the spirit. Declare all the good the Lord sees in them and all the good things He has in store for them. As you do, you will connect with God's heart, find yourself wanting only the very best for them, discover it is almost impossible to be angry or upset with them, and refuse division. It can't be a battle if you refuse to be an enemy!

Romans 12:14 tells us not to curse those who persecute us, but instead to bless them. When we speak curses, we empower Leviathan (Job 3:8). It wants us to feel persecuted and lash back. But when we choose to move in the opposite spirit and declare blessings over those who are persecuting us, we defang this wicked serpent. It can no longer inject its vile venom into us. Leviathan thrives by darting back and forth in a conversation, creating offense and bitterness on both sides. When we refuse to speak with its poisonous tongue, we shut the door to its manipulations on our side of the communications.

We love decrees in our ministry. We believe the Word when it says, "Decree a thing, and it will be established" (Job 22:28). We have seen the Word go forth and shift atmospheres, create realms, and defeat the enemy. And through the spoken Word, so will you.

(See the section on Additional Resources near the back of the book for powerful decree and prayer tools you can put to work on your behalf to secure victories and lay hold of promises.)

Key Seven:

PRAYER

When Leviathan is active, communication is an issue. As I have stressed throughout this book, words get twisted. Meaning and intent are misinterpreted. And usually the more we try to explain – the more words we use to try to communicate what we really mean – the more this spirit twists things. When Leviathan is rampant, the safest place for us to be communicating is with the Lord.

A ministry that I have a long-standing connection with asked me for counsel during an onslaught of Leviathan. One disagreement after another was breaking out amongst their usually tight-knit and loving team. At the height of all the misunderstandings, they were also dealing with an internal disciplinary issue with someone who was going through a process of repentance and restoration. One of their core team members who was involved in overseeing this process was taking a hard-lined punitive approach to disciplining the person under correction, leaving no room for possible reinstatement on the other side of repentance and restoration. I, along with the ministry leader, was not in agreement with this approach, mindset, and heart-posture.

We definitely saw the need for discipline and correction, but our perspective was that it should be unto the possibility of redemption. We not only wanted to help the people who had been wronged, we wanted to help the person who had made the mistakes. The more we tried to talk with the team member about this, the more Leviathan twisted it until all she was hearing was that we were against the people who had been hurt and were making excuses for the perpetrator. It got so bad that at one point this core team member accused the ministry leader and me of being against her, making her the villain, and not even seeing that the person under discipline had done wrong. The team member felt unheard, unvalued, and like she was the only one standing up for what was right. The more the other leader and I tried to explain and assure the team member that she was being heard and that her opinion mattered, the more Leviathan twisted it all and damaged relationship. At one point this team member who had served faithfully and diligently in this ministry for more than a decade was ready to throw everything away, resign, and never speak to the leader again.

We realized that our attempts to communicate were not working because Leviathan was so twisting and perverting all that we were saying. So we went into prayer, giving it all to the Lord, asking Him to open the eyes of all involved to see things how they truly were, declaring Holy Spirit was able to lead everyone into all truth no matter how temporarily murky and confused Leviathan had made things. In only a few days everything shifted. The Lord spoke directly to the team member, showing her an unhealed wound in her heart from when someone had done something wrong to her many years ago and was not held accountable. As soon as she saw it, she realized she had been acting out of that wound, causing her to be against the person we wanted to see redeemed. She realized that our being for this person in the discipline process did not mean we were against the ones who had been wronged, nor were we against her. Her heart changed imme-diately, and everything shifted. What could not be accomplished with our words in conversations over the course of almost two weeks was accomplished in just a few days through prayer. Thank You, Lord!

Observing what others have encountered in battles with Leviathan has helped me walk through and see victory in many of my own battles. I've learned much by watching team and group dynamics in the midst of Leviathan's chaos and confusion. And I must say, it is easier to deal with when you are outside the swirls than when you are inside of them.

Talk to God, Not About Others

If you are in the midst of a Leviathan assault, you are wiser to be on your knees than on the phone talking, texting, and telling everyone what you are going through; or on your computer send-ing emails and posting on social media; or at lunch rehashing for the umpteenth time with the umpteenth person how unfairly you have been treated. Go into prayer. Go to the Lord. Tell *Him* all that is happening. Pour out your heart to Him. And then take some time to listen to what He has to say.

Prayer is a two-way street. It is a conversation. And God more than likely has something to say that will be profoundly helpful in your situation. It was in prayer that our ministry received the keys in this book to help us overcome the Leviathan spirit when it assaulted our team. It was in prayer that the Lord helped me get past what would have been my initial knee-jerk carnal responses and opened my eyes to see things from His perspective. He spoke to me about how He would handle things. He showed me what love looked like, what true justice would be, and how I was to fight for (not against) the people involved in all the swirls and confusion. He wooed me past irritation and frustration into peace and faith-filled expectation. He gave my mentor and myself strategies to share with our staff, as well as wisdom to help us all keep watch over our hearts and words. During the worst of the attacks and swirls, much more was achieved and accomplished in prayer and devotional times with Him than in the meeting after meeting I had with people who were upset with one another.

Prayer helps get us out of our heads and into our hearts. Remember that Leviathan darts back and forth to create chaos and confusion on both sides of communications. That means that just as you have been misunderstood and misinterpreted by the other person, there is a very good chance that you have done the same to him or her. Leviathan wants you up in your head. It wants you rehearsing and rehashing all the horrible, unfair things you think have been said about you and done to you. Leviathan wants you dwelling on how difficult and dire the situation seems. Prayer brings you into the presence of the Prince of Peace. Prayer brings heavenly calm, divine insight, and breakthrough solutions.

In Acts 12 we find the enemy using Herod to come against the church. He was on a rampage against the disciples who were out preaching the Good News of Jesus Christ (Acts 12:1-3). He had Peter arrested and thrown in prison (v. 4). Herod's intent was to put Peter on trial and more than likely have him executed. It looked bad. The enemy was coming against the communication of the Gospel, persecuting believers, locking them up, and threatening their lives. What could the church possibly do? Pray! Which is exactly what they did. Instead of murmuring and complaining about it all, they prayed without ceasing (v. 5). Those prayers brought forth a sudden solution (v. 7) – an angel who went into the prison and set Peter free (vv. 7-10). Breakthrough! The next thing the church knew, Peter was a free man knocking at their door (v. 13). Because they prayed.

We sometimes diminish the importance of prayer or are dismissive about its impact. I sometimes hear people say, "Well, there is nothing we can do *but* pray." As if prayer was way down on the list of possible solutions, one to turn to only if nothing better can be thought of. Prayer is the first thing we should do. Prayer is what brings solutions. When we pray in faith, we become Kingdom-come conduits connecting earth to heaven, allowing us to bind the things of hell and loose the things of God so that the schemes of the enemy are rendered null and void. When we pray it opens the door for heaven to invade earth. Prayer works!

Key Eight:

PRAISE AND WORSHIP

Job 41:34 makes it clear that Leviathan is a king, and we have seen that this spirit wants to rule and reign. One of the easiest and most effective ways to dethrone Leviathan in any situation is to enthrone God. We do this, according to Psalm 22:3, by praising Him:

You are holy, O You who are enthroned upon the praises of [Your people].

When we praise and worship the Lord we not only welcome Him into the situation, we *enthrone* Him – giving Him place to rule and reign! Praise and worship is a beacon beamed out in the spirit that invites the King of Glory to come in. And who is the King of Glory? He is the Lord Almighty, the Lord invincible in battle, the Lord of Hosts (Psalm 24:8, 10). When we lift our voices to praise and worship the Lord in the midst of challenges beyond our abilities, things shift and change. How can they not? He is ALL mighty. He is INVINCIBLE. And He commands LEGIONS of ANGELS.

Sometimes when we are in a battle we get too focused on the enemy – what he's doing, how it's affecting us, the problems it's creating. If we're not careful, this will take us into a place of fear. Fear works like faith, only in a negative way. Job said, "What I fear comes upon me, and what I dread befalls me" (Job 3:25). Fear is a landing strip for the enemy. It draws him, gives him place, and empowers him. The more we focus on Leviathan and all the chaos, havoc, misunderstanding and miscommunication it is creating, the more we are prone to fear and frustration. Leviathan wants us afraid. It wants us frustrated. It wants us speaking out of anxiety, irritation, and aggravation. It wants us murmuring and complaining. It wants us cursing and speaking ill of one another. That is all fuel to its fire. But if we will shift our focus from what the enemy is doing back to who our God is, our circumstances will also shift.

Think of Paul and Silas in Acts 16. They had just cast a demon out of the witch girl (v. 18). Their "reward" for this good act was to be stripped, beaten, imprisoned in a dungeon, and thrown into stocks (vv. 22-24). Their situation was awful – and awfully unfair. But instead of focusing on all the negatives, they turned their focus to the Lord (v. 25). As they prayed, praised, and worshipped, the prison shook, their chains fell off, and the doors flew open (v. 26). All the prisoners were freed, and the jailer and his entire family got saved. Praise changes the atmosphere! Praise shifts things! Praise sets us free from the traps and schemes of the enemy!

As we praise and worship God, we are reminded who He is and what He is like. We are reminded of His greatness, His power, His might. We are reminded that He is the King of Kings, the Lord of Lords (Revelations 19:16), the God of Breakthrough (2 Samuel 5:20), and that He does not fail (Joshua 1:5). When we focus on Him with our praise, worship, and adoration, we draw Him who is Light (1 John 1:5) into the situation – no darkness, confusion, or chaos of Leviathan can stand. Our fear fades. Our frustration disappears. Our faith increases. Expectation of the victory that must come forth fills us. The next thing we know we are declaring and decreeing all that He is showing us *(remember the keys work together)*. That is the power of praise and worship.

Praise Even If You Don't Feel Like It!

If you have ever heard me preach, you have probably heard me say, "The Kingdom is simple, but it is not always easy." What I mean by this is that the tools, weapons, and keys the Lord has given us as new covenant believers are effective and they work when we use them – simple. The challenge is that oftentimes in the midst of a battle the toughest thing to do is the very thing we need to do most. In the midst of a maelstrom of confusion, misunderstanding, and miscommunication that Leviathan has stirred up, the easy thing to do is to take offense, be frustrated, speak negatively, and murmur and complain about how it seems the enemy is winning and God is nowhere to be found. The powerful thing to do is to praise, worship, and bring the Lord Almighty into the battle! Often the very best time to praise the Lord is when we least feel like it.

> *When we focus on Him with our praise, worship, and adoration, we draw Him who is Light (1 John 1:5) into the situation — no darkness, confusion, or chaos of Leviathan can stand.*

Key Nine:

FORGIVENESS

The enemy knows the power of unity. All of hell is aware that while one can put a thousand to flight, two can put ten thousand (Deuteronomy 32:30). There is a logarithmic progression of impact for the Kingdom when we link arms together and co-labor for the Lord. That's why Leviathan wants to set believer against believer, church against church, household against household. It wants to fracture and divide the Body so we are left angry, bitter, isolated, and wary of one another. How many precious believers are out there right now, forsaking fellowship and covering because they have been hurt by a church, a leader, or another believer? How many aren't connecting with ones they could be a blessing to or be blessed by, because they're locked up in offense and unforgiveness?

There is a reason God calls us into fellowship (Hebrews 10:24-25). It is the same reason the enemy tries to drive us apart. It is much easier for hell to come against believers one at a time, as opposed to when we are walking together in accountability, encouragement, exhortation, and edification. Even more, the enemy is aware that if he can turn believers against each other and stir us to think and speak ill of one another, then we actually do his work for him. Leviathan is one of his most cunning stealth agents working to divide believers, and unforgiveness is one of this spirit's greatest traps.

I once heard a powerful preacher say that unforgiveness is like "drinking poison, hoping that it kills your enemy." In other words, when we refuse to forgive we think we are punishing the one who did us wrong, but really we are only punishing ourselves. When we are in unforgiveness our hearts are hard, shutting us off from the flow of the Kingdom into our lives. We are coming into agreement with darkness instead of light.

The lie the enemy tells us about forgiveness is that if we forgive, we are saying that what was done to us (or said about us) was okay, that it was not wrong, that it was "no big deal." Forgiveness is not about excusing the actions of others; it is about removing the impact of those actions from our lives. When Jesus forgave us on the cross, He was not saying that sin was "no big deal," He was removing sin's ability to continue to separate us from our Heavenly Father and all of His Kingdom. Unforgiveness isolates us. It cuts us off. It keeps us from being who we were created – in love, by love, and for love – to be. But forgiveness, glorious Christlike forgiveness, plugs us into the heart of the Father, all that He is, and all that He has.

When Leviathan is active, hurts occur. When we are misunderstood, misrepresented, or lied about ... it *hurts*. But those wounds cannot begin to truly heal until we forgive. We must forgive those who did us wrong, and forgive ourselves for any wrong actions or words that we are guilty of. Proverbs 17:9 (NLT) says that love (and thus all the peace, joy, and hope that comes with it) prospers when a wrong is forgiven, but dwelling on a wrong will separate even the closest of friends. In other words: Forgiveness opens the door to healing and closes it on Leviathan.

Here is a prayer of forgiveness for you when Leviathan has been active in your midst:

Lord Jesus, by Your grace I forgive all others just as You have forgiven me. I forgive everyone who has misunderstood, misrepresented, or lied about me in any way. I forgive myself for any time that I have taken offense, or allowed anger and bitterness to enter into my heart. I apply Your blood to this entire situation, and ask that every wrong word I have spoken about anyone, or that has been spoken about me, would fall to the ground harmless and ineffective. I forgive all who have cursed me, and choose to bless them. May they know the fullness of Your love, acceptance, and comfort in all they are going through. In Your mighty name I pray, Jesus. Amen.

Key Ten:

WISDOM

One of the tricks of Leviathan is that it makes you think you know things that are not necessarily so. It will twist words and understanding, appealing to your old prideful, carnal nature to convince you that the person with whom you are caught in its swirl has wicked motives and evil intent toward you. It will hiss lies into your ear that you are "discerning" something about your "enemy," when in truth what is really happening is this foul spirit is passing off misinformation as perceived fact. This is why it is critical that we cry out to God for His true wisdom in the midst of Leviathan's manipulations and machinations.

Proverbs 4:6 promises that divine wisdom will protect and watch over us. Ecclesiastes 2:26 shows us that when God gives wisdom, true knowledge and happiness come with it. And James 1:5 makes it clear that when we need wisdom – when we need to know what God's thoughts, insights, and approach would be in any given situation – all we have to do is ask and He will gladly tell us.

During Leviathan's onslaught against our ministry, there were many times I needed to seek God for wisdom. I would ask, "Lord, what is the best course of action here?" "What will achieve the greatest good?" Or even better, the question my friend and mentor has taught me to ask, "Lord, what does love look like in these circumstances?" No matter how contentious or difficult things got at times, no matter how much my flesh was crying out to lash back or retaliate in a given moment, if I was willing to quiet myself and approach the Lord knowing He had an answer, He was always able to lift His voice up above the din of the confusion and chaos (Psalm 46:10). What I have learned is that there can be responses, actions, and choices that seem right, that might even feel right; but if they do not come with the peace of the Lord, if they do not look and sound like love, if they do not seek the good of the other person as much as the good of our self, then they are not the wisdom of God.

In John 5:19 Jesus declares that He does nothing on His own, but only does what He sees His Father do. That word "sees" in the Greek is *blepo* and it means "to behold or perceive." The word "do" or "does" in that Scripture is the Greek *poieo* which can be translated as "agree," "abide" or "band together." So Jesus is revealing to us that He abides in His Father, walking as one with Him in agreement, doing only what He beholds or perceives His Father would do. He is perfectly representing the Father in all things at all times (Colossians 1:15, Hebrews 1:3). He then goes on to declare that it is not His words that He speaks, but only words the Father has given Him (John 12:49). He only did what the Father showed Him to do, and only spoke words the Father gave Him to speak. He was the perfect embodiment of the wisdom of God in all situations at all times. That is why everywhere He went, every demon and demonic plot was defeated.

This is how Jesus lived when He was on the earth, and because of Him it is how we can live here now. Seek God and His wisdom in any confusing and chaotic situation you find yourself in. Before you speak or act and potentially make things worse, take some time to tuck into Him and allow Him to teach you how to be "wise as serpents, and harmless as doves (KJV)." That quote is from Matthew 10:16, when Jesus was commissioning His most trusted disciples to go out and change the world. He told them that He was sending them out "as sheep in the midst of wolves." He knows there is wickedness and viciousness in the fallen world and that they will wrestle with powers and principalities that want to devour them and distract them from their assignment to advance His Kingdom. They will not be able to overcome the enemy in their own strength, but they will not have to! He is giving them the key: Go as sheep, for sheep hear their shepherd's voice. In other words, in all things at all times we must listen for Him, for He will speak to us and give us wisdom – divine wisdom that empowers us to be wise as serpents and harmless as doves.

Serpents are very aware of their environment. They wait for just the right moment and then they strike. The wisdom of God helps us to discern what is truly going on and empowers us to move efficiently and effectively against the enemy and his schemes. Be still. Take your time to hear from the Lord. Then move with intention. When we have the wisdom of God we will strike down the enemy and yet have no harm in our hearts toward the people involved. The end result will be like when the Lord commended the disciples for their effectiveness against the enemy, saying, "I saw Satan fall from heaven like lightning!" (Luke 10:18 NLT). The enemy was overcome, and the disciples had learned how to wield the power the Lord had equipped them with – power over all the authority of the enemy!

Key Eleven:

ADVISORS

According to Proverbs 11:14 (KJV), in the multitude of counselors there is safety. This is definitely true when you are under assault by Leviathan. When this spirit is at work, communications get distorted, understanding gets murky, and you begin to question just about everything. It can be overwhelming, which is why it helps to have "fresh" eyes and ears. Seeking counsel from trusted and experienced advisors who are outside of the conflicts, swirls, and situations you are in the midst of can provide critical insights and a calming influence.

Our ministry has multiple layers of covering and accountability. One of them is a group of respected apostolic leaders who all have decades of experience in ministry. When dealing with the Leviathan assault within our ranks, we reached out to several of these advisors. We shared with them, as objectively as possible, what was happening in the natural and in the spirit. We also invited them to speak with the others involved in the situations, so they could hear directly from them as well. Because these advisors were outside of all the confusion that Leviathan was stirring up inside our ministry, they were able to see things clearly and bring counsel that helped cut through the bewilderment, and also confirm what we were hearing from the Lord. They were able to speak truth to the different parties involved and be heard and understood much more easily because they were not within the main swirls of Leviathan's attack. Their advice, counsel, and assistance played an important part in helping to dispel the chaos of Leviathan's distortions and restoring clarity to our understanding and communications.

Think of King David in 2 Samuel 19. After a lengthy and difficult season of wrestling with his son Absalom, David was not thinking clearly. Their relationship had been mired in hurt, misunderstanding, offense, bitterness, rejection, and betrayal. Despite David's best efforts to reach out and bring restoration, things had gone from bad to worse. Absalom schemed and plotted against his father, inciting a revolt that deposed David as king (2 Samuel 15:13-14). He then pursued David with tens of thousands of troops with the intention of killing him and securely establishing the throne as his own (2 Samuel 17:24). During the battle, Absalom lost his life (2 Samuel 18:15). Despite all the schemes, betrayals, attacks, and anger over the many years of their contentious relationship, David, of course, grieved the death of his son (2 Samuel 18:33). But the grief got twisted into something more than sadness over the loss. It became dysfunctional. It affected everyone around him, including his many troops who had fought well and valiantly on his behalf (2 Samuel 19:2). In fact, David's reaction made them feel so bad, these valiant, loyal troops "crept

Seeking counsel from trusted and experienced advisors who are outside of the conflicts, swirls, and situations you are in the midst of can provide critical insights and a calming influence.

back into the town that day as though they were ashamed and had deserted in battle" (v. 3 NLT). David was so lost in the swirls of his hurt that he was not able to clearly see how it was negatively impacting him, his brave warriors, and his kingdom (v. 4). It took a trusted advisor to help him see how twisted it had all become (vv. 5-6), and to give him wise counsel on how to set it all straight (vv. 7-8).

The Lord says that when we need wisdom, all we have to do is ask Him and He will generously provide it (James 1:5). One of the ways He can do this in the midst of the swirling assaults of Leviathan is by giving wise counsel through trusted advisors outside the situation.

Key Twelve:

RECONCILIATION AND RESTORATION

When Jesus went to the cross on our behalf, He not only defeated all of hell and death, He reconciled our sins and restored us to relationship with our Heavenly Father and His Kingdom. He put back into place all that we had before the Fall. Our God is not only a warrior who provides victory over the enemy, He is also a reconciler and restorer who puts everything right.

Think of Job. When all was said and done, the Lord not only led him into victory over the enemy but also drew Job into a closer and more intimate relationship with Him (Job 42:5). Plus He restored Job's fortunes so that he was doubly blessed (Job 42:10, 12). This is who our God is. This is what it looks like when the enemy is defeated and divine justice is achieved.

When Leviathan is at work, things get messy. Communications get messy. Emotions get messy. Relationships get messy. Things are said and done in frustration, irritation, and hurt that should not have been said or done. The ultimate defeat of Leviathan is not just overcoming its schemes and clearing its chaos and confusion from our midst. Truly overcoming this spirit involves doing all we can to make things right. It is important to go to people and apologize for wrong attitudes you had or wrong words you spoke during the conflict. Don't wait for them to come to you. Start the process. And if by chance they do not respond in kind, don't hold it against them. Remember, we don't do the right thing to get a right result; we do the right thing because He who is righteous lives inside of us. When you put things right on your end – when you do all you can to reconcile and restore everything to how it was before Leviathan's assault – you are fully closing the door on that twisted spirit.

The Key:

THE SPIRIT OF CHRIST

Before I end this section on the keys to overcoming the spirit of Leviathan, I want to ask you a question. Do you see a common denominator among all the keys? They all look and sound like Christ. They all embrace and embody His character and nature. When we choose to walk *like* Him, we are empowered to walk *as* Him (John 14:12, John 20:21).

Holy Spirit is well able to meet and mentor us in any situation. Even in the midst of a twisted, swirling onslaught of the spirit of Leviathan, Holy Spirit can clearly speak to us and help us walk, talk, think, and act like Christ.

An excellent strategy in any spiritual warfare is to move in the opposite spirit of whatever darkness is coming against you. There is nothing more completely and totally opposite of the spirit of Leviathan than the Spirit of Christ.

4

THE BATTLE IS THE LORD'S

Whenever I find myself in a season of warfare, I like to get into the Old Testament. It is filled with battles where the Lord leads His people into victory against impossible odds. I find all these stories very insightful and encouraging. The book of Joshua is one of my absolute favorites. Especially where the Lord reminds Joshua that no enemy will be able to stand their ground against him for as long as he lives because the Lord will always be with him and will never fail or abandon him (Joshua 1:5). Also, where He tells Joshua there is no need to ever be afraid or discouraged, for God is with him wherever he goes (Joshua 1:9). Wow! Talk about a faith boost in the midst of a battle.

With that in mind, I want to look at one other passage of Scripture about Leviathan. In Job 41 it says:

If you lay a hand on it, you will remember the struggle and never do it again! Any hope of subduing it is false; the mere sight of it is overpowering. ... When it rises up, the mighty are terrified; they retreat before its thrashing. The sword that reaches it has no effect, nor does the spear or the dart or the javelin. Iron it treats like straw and bronze like rotten wood. Arrows do not make it flee; slingstones are like chaff to it. A club seems to it but a piece of straw; it laughs at the rattling of the lance. ... Nothing on earth is its equal.

—*Job 41:8-9, 25-29, 33 (NIV)*

On the surface that may not sound very encouraging or give you a big faith boost. After all, it seems to be saying that if we try to go against the terrifying, mighty Leviathan we will regret it because none of our weapons can touch it and nothing on earth is its equal. What chance do little old you and me have against something so powerful? Well, *every* chance. Because it is not just little old you and me going up against Leviathan. It is little old you and me in Christ, with Christ, and for Christ going up against it. The weapons of our warfare against this spirit are not carnal (steel, iron, wood, and stone) but mighty spiritual weapons in God that He has equipped and empowered us with to tear down powers and principalities like Leviathan (2 Corinthians 10:4).

I believe that this passage in Job is reminding us that, left to ourselves and in our own strength, it would be a mistake to go up against a demonic power like Leviathan. But we are not left to ourselves, and we need not (and should not) battle in our own strength. Like Joshua, we have a word from the Lord that He who has all authority in heaven and earth is always with us wherever we go (Matthew 28:18, 20). On top of that, the Lord has given us authority over all the power of the enemy (Luke 10:19), has outfitted us with heavenly armor and weaponry (Ephesians 6:13-18), and He will always bring us into victory (2 Corinthians 2:14). In other words, we do not need to be afraid of Leviathan; it needs to be afraid of those who are walking with the Lord. How about that for some encouragement?!

Think of King Jehoshaphat (2 Chronicles 20). He was beset by not one, not two, but three enemy forces. They were all marching against him. In the natural it looked hopeless, impossible even. Jehoshaphat knew he was powerless against the might of the enemy massed against him, and had no idea what to do ... except turn to the Lord (v. 12). God's response was to say, "Do not be afraid. Don't be discouraged by the might of the enemy, for the battle is not yours, but the Lord's" (v. 15). He then went on to tell Jehoshaphat that while the battle was the Lord's, it was important that his people take their position on the battlefield, stand still, and watch the Lord's victory (v. 17). The next day they did as instructed by God. The result was that they saw the enemy utterly destroyed, and it took them three days to collect all the spoils of the victory!

It is the same in any battle we face. Especially with a powerful principality like Leviathan. On the surface, this spirit looks just like it says in Job 41 – mighty, terrifying, overwhelming, and such that none of our natural approaches (weapons) will have any effect on it. In the midst of an onslaught of Leviathan we can feel like Jehoshaphat did at first – overwhelmed, powerless, and afraid. But the "recipe" the Lord gave him for victory against crushing odds in his day will also work for us in ours, because the Lord is the same yesterday, today, and forever (Hebrews 13:8, Malachi 3:6):

1. ***Do Not Be Afraid or Discouraged*** (2 Chronicles 20:15): In other words, get your soul under control! Leviathan wants to stir you into reacting (and overreacting). When this spirit is coming against you, you will feel misunderstood,

maligned, accused, offended, and a variety of other emotions and reactions. You will feel like lashing out, retaliating, speaking ill of others, giving up, and throwing in the towel. Don't. The righteous do not live by feelings, they live by faith (Romans 1:17). Don't place faith in your ability to straighten out the twistings of Leviathan; it will only get you frustrated and discouraged. Place your faith in the Lord. Come out of agreement with – and repent of – any anger, frustration, bitterness, negativity, offense, or pride you have allowed to get hold of you. Give it all over to the Lord, and enter into His rest. Praise and worship your way into knowing and declaring that no matter how things might look or feel, greater is He!

2. ***Know that the Battle is the Lord's*** (2 Chronicles 20:15): Rejoice that the battle is the Lord's AND that He has won. Jesus Christ defeated all of hell and death at the Cross of Calvary (Revelation 1:18). There is not one work or minion of the enemy that He has not utterly overcome (1 John 3:8) and made a spectacle of (Colossians 2:15) – including Leviathan. Meditate on these and other key Scriptures that have been cited throughout this book until you *know that you know* that the enemy is defeated. We do not contend *for* victory, we contend *from* victory!

3. ***Take Your Position*** (2 Chronicles 20:17): Your position is in Christ (Ephesians 2:6; John 15:5) – inside of the complete, utter and total victory of the Cross. Stand in faith, praising and worshipping the Lord for what He has done and what He is about to bring forth.

4. *Stand Still* (2 Chronicles 20:17): Do not be budged by what you see or feel. Remain in faith, no matter what. Do not waver or doubt (James 1:6-8). If you find that you have, simply repent, ask God for a greater grace, and enter back into that place of faith (Hebrews 3:14; 4:9-10).

5. ***Watch for the Lord's Victory*** (2 Chronicles 20:17): Be expectant in your faith. When you know that you have triumphed through the Cross, it helps you see the victory and expect it to come forth. I often tell people that when it comes to the promises of God, we are not contending for something we might have one day, we are contending for the full manifestation of what we *know* is ours. Our faith is a substance (Hebrews 11:1) that makes manifest what God has already given us. Get in the Word. Read and meditate on passages of Scripture where the Lord brought forth victory. Let Him build your faith so that you see the victory, knowing Leviathan is defeated and that you are about to collect the spoils!

We cannot take Leviathan out in our own strength. But praise the Lord, we don't have to. The battle is the Lord's, and He has already won it for us. We get to legislate that victory – decreeing and declaring it – until we see Leviathan taken out through the finished work of the Cross!

5

YOU WILL RECOVER ALL

We have seen that Leviathan is a demonic king that desires to rule and reign (Job 41:34). It wants to take and usurp "territory" – spheres of influence, key relationships, strategic alliances, areas of strength. It does this by creating miscommunication, misunderstanding, confusion, and chaos to catch people up in offense, bitterness, anger, and irritation so that we turn on one another – breaking unity, and using the authority of our words to sow division and discord. This spirit knows the power of united believers (in churches, marriages, families, businesses, schools, workplaces, homes, and ministries), which is why it works so hard to set them against one another. The end result is broken relationships and lost opportunities.

As you have been reading this book, I am sure you have had situations come to mind when there were assaults against you and your territory. Assaults marked by swirls of confusion and miscommunication that made you feel misunderstood and maligned – where the harder you worked to straighten things out, the more twisted it all became. At the time, you may not have realized that it was something much more than a "flesh and blood" misunderstanding, but now your eyes have been opened. Now you know that these situations were assaults by a demonic power. And now that you realize that you have been stolen from, it is time to take back your territory.

The enemy may have taken you by surprise, but he never takes God by surprise. The Lord is well able to guide you and lead you into taking back all that was stolen. Do not be afraid that anything has been permanently lost; instead, rejoice in the revelation that all will be restored!

You are not the first to face a situation like this. In 1 Samuel 29, David was rejected by the company he had been serving with. Despite having a sterling record of success and loyalty (v. 3), all of a sudden he was doubted, mistrusted, and shunned (v. 4). David was confused, felt misunderstood, and though he tried to explain his side of it, he was still sent away – he lost his place as well as one of the most important strategic alliances in his life at that time (vv. 8-10).

If that wasn't bad enough, when David returned to the village where he lived, he and the men who were still with him discovered that the enemy had raided their camp, stolen all of their possessions, kidnapped all of their families and relations, and burned the place to the ground (1 Samuel 30:1-2). The enemy had taken everything. Emotions were high, bitterness and offense were rampant, and David's remaining men turned on him – they were even discussing stoning him (v. 6). It looked dire. David was distressed, but instead of giving in to despair and defeat, he turned to the Lord (v. 6). When he did, this is what he was told: "Pursue, for you shall surely overtake them and without fail recover all"

(v. 8 NKJV). In other words, don't give up, go after the enemy, and expect total recompense!

When David embraced the "keys" the Lord gave him, he and his men saw their unity restored (v. 9), received a divine appointment that gave them necessary strategic insight and information (v. 11-16), slaughtered the enemy (v. 17), and took back all that had been stolen, including all of their relationships (v. 18). Nothing was missing (v. 19). They recovered all.

There is one other thing I want to point out from this story that has special relevance in regards to the spirit of Leviathan. Much of the division and loss that was created along the way came from misunderstanding, mistrust, offense, and bitterness (1 Samuel 29:3, 4-6, 8; 1 Samuel 30:6). David leaned into the Lord for answers to it all. He ended up seeing total victory and having all restored. On top of that, when the enemy tried to get back in and create mistrust and offense among David's men after the victory (1 Samuel 30:22), David quickly took authority over it and squashed it before it could take root (1 Samuel 30:23-24). Do you see it? David not only saw all restored, he also had grown in authority. All the enemy had stolen was recovered, *and* David now was treading upon the twisted serpent, crushing its head, and driving it from his camp!

Now that your eyes are open to the workings of Leviathan, you can see where it has come against you and what it has stolen or destroyed. There is nothing it has taken that cannot be recovered. Through this book, the Lord has given you insight, understanding, and keys that will help you overcome Leviathan. Use them to pursue, overtake, and recover all – *and* to drive Leviathan from your midst if it tries to rear its head again.

The enemy may try to convince you that your situation is too big, the defeat too great, or the wound too old. It may look and feel that way, but none of that is true. It is just the spirit of Leviathan hissing lies at you. Remember the Cross of Calvary! To all the world at the time, the Cross looked like a great defeat – the end of Jesus. It was anything but! Within what appeared to natural eyes and understanding as a defeat was the greatest triumph ever, where Jesus recovered all – all people and all creation for all time!

What may look or feel like a great defeat to you actually contains the seeds of a great victory. You will recover all!

In Joel 2:25 (NLT) the Lord promises, "I will give you back what you lost."

In Isaiah 61:7, He promises that He will not only restore but will bring you into double! And in Isaiah 61:3 (NIV), He promises that He will give you "beauty" for "ashes." So anything and anywhere that Leviathan has taken from you, expect payback, expect double, and expect it to be better than before. YAY, GOD!!

It is time to recover all that the enemy has stolen. Grab hold of the keys the Lord has given you through this book and put them to work. Let your spirit arise! Let the Lion who dwells within you roar! Declare right now, *"I WILL RECOVER ALL!"*

ADDITIONAL TOOLS
AND RESOURCES

FIRE POWER PRAYER PLUNGE

Are you ready to add some FIRE Power to your prayer life? These ten power-packed messages are like being personally mentored by Robert Hotchkin and Patricia King in all manner of prayer. Learn how to pray like Elijah prayed, and how to get the same results – glorious harvest and radical revival!

VICTORY!

Our God is invincible. All might, all power, and all authority are His. He never loses, and He wants to help you lay hold of certain victory and equip you to take down the giants in the land so that you can inhabit all of His promises and see all of His blessings! At the end of this message, Robert Hotchkin prays for the Spirit of the Overcomer to be released to you.

DIVINE UNION:
DECREES FOR A HEAVENLY MARRIAGE

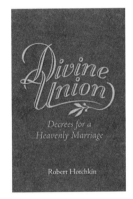

Whether you're believing to meet your special someone, are on your way to the altar with the one the Lord has for you, or are currently married but want to strengthen your relationship – God's desire is to co-labor with you to bring about the marriage you have always wanted. Put the decrees in this book to work on your behalf and watch as all of heaven moves to bring you into a supernatural marriage framed by His Word and filled with His blessings.

DECREE: THIRD EDITION

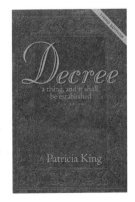

The expanded *Decree: Third Edition* helps believers activate the power of the Word in key areas of their lives, including health, provision, love, victory, wisdom, family, business, blessing, favor, and more. New decrees in this edition are "Great Grace," Rejuvenation," "12 Decrees for Your Nation," and "I Am Supernatural in Christ."

RESTING IN GOD

If you've ever wondered why God allows us to face challenges beyond our understanding, this message will bring you peace and launch you into a new place of security in God where nothing hell sends against you will cause you fear or anxiety ever again. Get ready to enter God's rest and know victory in every circumstance you face.

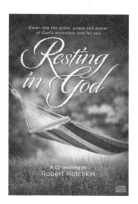

YOU ARE SUPERNATURAL!

Jesus promises that we will truly do the works that He did, and greater works. If we believe. Nowhere in the Word does it say we have to feel supernatural to be supernatural. It simply says we have to believe. This message will stir your faith that you, yes you, are a miracle-working releaser-of-heaven waiting to happen. Your past doesn't disqualify you. Your mistakes don't disqualify you. Nothing disqualifies you, if you believe!

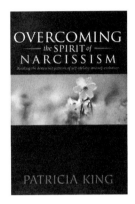

Available at the Store at **XPministries.com**

YOUR GOD-GIVEN IDENTITY

You have a God-given identity the Lord wants to reveal to you. This message reveals the power of living from who you were created to be, plus how to avoid allowing the enemy, those around you, or even yourself to steal or weaken the impact and power of your God-given  identity. Bring an end to spiritual identity theft!

ENGAGING WITH GOD

You are God's beloved child, and there is nothing He wants more than to draw you into the fullness of His love and engage you in a lifestyle of never-ending intimacy. Truly knowing the Lord in this place of deep communion is the key to living a Kingdom life. Robert exposes the lies of  the enemy that separate us from God, and reveals how simple it is to fully respond to the Lord's invitation to know Him intimately and engage with Him powerfully.

MORE!

Have you been crying out for more of God? More of His presence? More revelation? More of His power? More of His Kingdom coming? More love? More miracles? More signs and wonders? Just … MORE!! Guess what? The Lord wants you to have it even more than you do! In this message, Robert prophesies, preaches, and reveals what the Lord is doing in the earth to unlock the amazing move of God that is coming, and how you can be a part of it!

SEEING MIRACLES

God is the Great I Am. He is the same for you today as He was for the New Testament apostles and the great revivalists. He is the same for you right where you are as He is in all the places around the world that miracles are breaking out. Discover how you can position yourself to see God move in amazing ways in your life. Don't settle for anything less than the miraculous, because the fullness of the Kingdom is for YOU and it is for NOW.!

ABOUT THE AUTHOR

In November of 2002, Robert Hotchkin was splitting wood in the mountains of Montana when he was radically saved and forever changed by the first of many encounters with the love of Jesus. He went from being a mocker and persecutor of Christians to a passionate lover of Christ. That passion for the Lord marks his ministry, and it is truly contagious. Robert travels the world, ministering with strong faith, releasing revelation, prophetic decrees, healings, miracles, and the love of God. He is a carrier of the glory and a sparker of revival fires. People have been healed, refreshed, set free, and empowered through his life. His great desire is that every person, city, nation, and region would know that God is good and that He really, really loves them!

Robert lives in Arizona with his wife Yu-Ree. Connect with him online and through social media so that he can continue to pour into you:

Twitter:	RobHotchXP
Facebook:	"Robert Hotchkin" + "Robert Hotchkin II"
Instagram:	Robert Hotchkin
YouTube:	Robert Hotchkin Channel
XPmedia.com:	Robert Hotchkin Channel (XPmedia.com/channel/rhotchkin)

Additional copies of this book and other
resources from Robert Hotchkin, as well as
other XP Publishing books, are available from
the online store at XPministries.com

**Wholesale prices for stores
and ministries**

Please contact:
resourcemanager@XPministries.com

www.XPministries.com
XP Ministries